Maud Blair was born to
English father and spent all
attended the University Co
to the UK, where she com
and Ethnic Studies at the University of Warwick followed by
a PhD in the Sociology of Education at the Open University.
There she worked for twelve years leading on courses in Race
and Education and Gender and Education. She then worked
as a civil servant in the Department for Education for three
years and as a consultant for The Learning Trust in Hackney
before she retired. Maud has three children and eight
grandchildren and lives in Cambridge.

'An important and powerful read, thank you Maud for your
vulnerability and honesty.'

Natalie Evans, author of *The Mixed-Race
Experience* and co-founder of Everyday Racism

'In telling her story, so that her children and grandchildren
might know, [Maud] unpeels the human cost of racism. I won't
be the only reader who marvels at the writer's resilience and
how she holds onto humanity in such a dehumanising society.'

Beverley Naidoo, acclaimed
author of *Journey to Jo'burg*

'Maud's autobiography is captivating, written in very read-
able prose. It's lucid, flowing and so warm.'

Ibbo Mandaza, Director of the SAPES Trust

'Blair paints a gripping, at times funny and harrowing picture of growing up in 1950s–1960s Rhodesia. A masterclass
in portraying what links identity, family and belonging in
this immensely enjoyable memoir. Originally written for her
grandchildren, this book will engage any and every reader.'

Professor Iram Siraj, University of Oxford

With special thanks to Basil Williams for their generous
support as a patron of this book

In Between

Maud Blair

unbound

First published in 2024

Unbound
c/o TC Group, 6th Floor Kings House, 9–10 Haymarket,
London, United Kingdom, SW1Y 4BP
www.unbound.com

Epigraph from *Race, Colour and Class in Southern Africa* (1997)
published with permission of the author, Ibbo Mandaza.

Typeset by Jouve (UK), Milton Keynes

A CIP record for this book is available from the British Library

ISBN 978-1-80018-293-6 (paperback)
ISBN 978-1-80018-292-9 (ebook)

Printed in Great Britain by Clays Ltd, Elcograf S.p.A.

This book is dedicated to my mother Serina Hakata, my Aunt Hilda, and my sister Margaret Crofts.

For my grandchildren so that they never forget.

Introduction

Throughout the book I use the term Coloured to describe people of mixed heritage (largely meaning white European with other ethnic groups) in Southern Africa. This is the term that was used since colonial times and is still used today. Any other terms such as black or African to describe people of mixed or dual heritage would, in the telling of the story, cause confusion about a country whose cultures and politics during colonial times were entirely defined by the superficial division of the population on the basis of skin colour or ethnic heritage. These imposed divisions determined one's place in the political, racial and social hierarchy and therefore determined one's life.

Where I use the term 'mixed heritage' this reflects the older me now living in the UK, deliberately avoiding the term Coloured and commenting about a particular situation as opposed to telling the story. The term 'people of colour' is used in context to describe all people who are not white.

The term Coloured is capitalised to reflect its use as an ethnic group in the same way that the labels African and European were used in Rhodesia. It is not equivalent to 'black' and 'white', which are used interchangeably with African and European and which I have not capitalised as, in this context, they simply describe the colour of a person.

For the social and political history of Rhodesia and Zimbabwe, I drew extensively from the following sources: Reginald Austin's *Racism and Apartheid in Southern Africa: Rhodesia, a book of data* (UNESCO Press, 1975), Ibbo Mandaza's *Race, Colour and Class in Southern Africa* (SAPES Books, 1997) and James Muzondidya's *Walking a Tightrope: Towards a Social History of the Coloured People of Zimbabwe* (Africa World Press, 2005).

Maud Blair

The particular statutes which referred specifically to 'Coloureds' had a two-fold purpose: firstly to separate them from Whites on the one hand and from Blacks on the other; and secondly to ensure by such separation that any threat to white privilege by persons of mixed race might be pre-empted while at the same time according the latter concessions designed to give them advantages not enjoyed by 'Natives'.

Ibbo Mandaza

One

My feet hurt. My shoes, new and brown and shiny, squeeze and pinch my toes and slice the backs of my ankles with each hurried step. I want to stop and kick them off but Amaiguru Hilda won't hear of it.

'Eeh! Don't be silly, Maudie. You can't wear a new dress and go to a big station full of people without any shoes on.'

I don't ask again. I think of our cows back home getting milked and having their legs bound together to stop them wandering off. I picture them longing to roam around freely, straining against the tightness of the cords that hold them still, and my chest tightens. I know now how they must feel. Except worse, because I can't even stand still, not with Amaiguru walking so quickly. How can she go so fast in her shoes, all pointy and high and sounding *ko ko ko ko* on the ground as she moves? *She must be even stronger than the cows*, I think. I grip her hand and try not to look scared.

It is night-time, but it's even brighter here in the train station in Salisbury than in the village when the moon is big and round and shiny and we all go to someone's house where we make a big circle and clap our hands and sing. Someone plays the drums and we dance under the full moon. Most of the grown-ups sit and watch but sometimes some of them join in.

There are lots of people in the station and the noise is deafening. They scatter and run this way and that, squawking and flapping and trampling everything in their path as they rush about, the way our chickens do when we go into the coop to try and catch one for our meal. Even the baby ones, which wouldn't even have enough meat on them for one person, join in the commotion. *We're like those chickens now.* As Amaiguru and I weave our way through the din, I feel suddenly guilty and sad. Sorry, chickens, I say in my head.

Some of the grown-ups around us are holding children's hands and tugging them along too, the way Amaiguru Hilda is pulling me; some are just standing and talking, some are on the big train beside us, looking out of the window like they forgot something. The station goes on for ever. *If Amaiguru lets go of my hand, I'll get lost and she'll never find me. Then I would never see my mummy again or play with my brother or my friends in the village. I would never see a bird or a cow or a moon in the sky again. There isn't even a tree in this place. And the roof is so high it might even be touching the sky. Imagine if I could climb right up to the top! My friends in the village would all wish they could be me.*

Amaiguru is holding my hand tightly. I am not sure what I'll do if she takes me on the train. It's very long, like lots of buses joined together. *It might even leave the station while we are still on it and then how will we get back?*

I'm walking with my eyes turned upwards, so I don't notice that Amaiguru has stopped until I bump into the back of her legs. She is talking to a lady dressed in funny clothes. *A white lady.* Most of the other white ladies in the station are dressed normally like Amaiguru, with their hats and their skirts and blouses and their *ko ko ko* shoes. But this lady is covered up in white from her head to her feet so that you can only see her face and hands and she doesn't have those high shoes. I think she's one of those people who takes naughty children to the factory where they turn them into corned beef. All the children in the village are scared to be taken to the white man's factory, because someone even found a finger inside the corned beef tin. A funny feeling wiggles through my stomach. My free hand starts to feel for something behind Amaiguru's back to hold on to and my heart is pounding inside my chest the way it does when I'm in trouble with Amai and praying I won't get clapped. I creep behind Amaiguru and hope that the strange white lady can't see me. I don't want to be turned into corned beef. Amaiguru is still chatting to the lady. I don't know what they are saying to each other because I only know how to speak chiZezuru, a dialect of the Shona language.

They stop talking.

Amaiguru bends down and picks up the case containing my new clothes, which she had put on the ground. She hands it to the white lady. *Why is she giving her my things?* A lump that feels like a hard stone fills my throat. I try to swallow it, but it won't go down. My fists curl into tight balls and my face feels hot. *Why did Amaiguru Hilda bring me all this way into town to buy me all of those new clothes if she was just planning to give them away to this strange person?*

I want to shout, *Please don't give away my new clothes*, but I know it is rude to talk when grown-ups are talking. I don't want to get clapped for being cheeky, but I plan to tell Amai about this when we get back to the village. Amai will not be happy that Amaiguru bought me new clothes, only to give them away.

Amaiguru reaches back and begins to pull me from behind her, but I hold onto her legs as tightly as I can.

'Come Maudie, come and see the Seesta,' she says.

7

What is Amaiguru talking about? I know that word because Stan taught me. He said that I am his seesta. So whose seesta is she? Surely not Amaiguru's – my mummy is Amaiguru's seesta; this is a white lady, a real murungu. *A* murungu *with funny clothes. She is not Amaiguru's seesta and she is not my seesta either. I don't know what Amaiguru means.*

The murungu lady stretches her arms to me and takes hold of my wrist. I scream. She tugs me by one arm as I try to cling to Amaiguru's leg with the other. Amaiguru helps her, peeling my arm away from her leg and forcing it into the Seesta's firm grip. The Seesta picks me up. I howl and stretch out my arms for my Amaiguru to take me back, kicking my skinny legs against the Seesta, who is struggling to hold on to me. Amaiguru strokes my face and says something to me, but when she gets closer, I fling my arms around her neck.

'*Musandisiye, Amaiguru! Musandisiye!*'

I'm hysterical. I don't let go. The Seesta is saying something to Amaiguru, who takes my hands, kisses my palms and then turns around suddenly and walks away. Panic-stricken, I feel certain that I am about to be taken to the white man's factory.

I watch my auntie disappear and, filled with pure terror, I scream so loudly that I can't hear any more noise from the station. 'Amai! Amai!' I wail, my arms still reaching out for my auntie, but this time crying for my Amai. My head hurts, my chest hurts, my whole body hurts. I go limp when the white lady carries me onto the train and lays me on the seat, all the while stroking my head and talking to me in a singsong and whispery voice. Someone comes to sit next to me. I can tell that it is not the lady in the funny clothes because the lady's clothes make a *shwe shwe* sound when she moves. *Maybe Amaiguru has changed her mind and has come to take me home.* I lift my head and look up.

It's a white girl with long, light-coloured hair done into

two plaits that hang on either side of her neck. She is not as white as the Seesta in the funny clothes. She is about the same height as my sister Abigail, only a lot thinner. She strokes my head and her voice is soft like feathers. She keeps saying 'shh, shh' over and over. I curl my body into the smallest ball. Even though it's quite warm in the train I can't stop shaking.

Then I remember something and I stop crying. '*Ndinoda mombe yangu*,' I say, looking hopefully at the kind girl sitting near me. Before I left the village, my brother Stan had carved a little cow for me from river clay so that I wouldn't forget him while I was in the big city. It's my special little *mombe* and I want it. It will make me feel better. '*Ndinoda mombe yangu*,' I ask again several times, but no one understands me. As I give in to exhaustion and fall asleep, I am certain of two things: I will never see my mummy again, and I am going to die.

I am four years old.

Two

It was, according to the nuns, at least a year before I said a single word. Life had seemed simple, safe, uncomplicated and predictable until the day Amaiguru Hilda appeared and told my mother that I had to go to school. My life, until then, had, like those of the rest of the village, revolved around the family, our fields, our cattle and our community. Our homestead was next to my great-uncle's. He was the local Headman. I loved Sekuru Marondera and spent hours following him around, helping him weed his small garden or simply sitting with him by the fire outside his house enjoying his stories. He was a tall man and thin – the fat seemed to have melted away in the hot sun, leaving just muscle, gristle and bone. He always stood upright, making him look taller than most men in the village, and, although the Headman, his face was not stern but gentle with a quick laugh and ready smile.

Sekuru would sit on a rock under the *muhacha* tree holding court or listening to supplicants who came and crouched down at a suitably respectful distance and clapped their hands to show respect, men curving their backs slightly and leaning their heads to one side, and women kneeling. He was the grandson of Chief Marondera, whose people inhabited the land in and around the modern town of Marandellas, as it was called by the European settlers, whose heavy tongues struggled to pronounce Marondera.

When the Rhodesian government introduced the Land Apportionment Act in 1930, the country was divided almost equally between land owned by white people and land owned by black people, despite the huge discrepancy in numbers, with white people constituting only 1 per cent of the total population in the country at that time. The best land was allocated for white settlement and the bulk of the productive, arable land was given to white farmers. My great-grandfather Marondera, who was the father of Sekuru Marondera, and his people were evicted from their ancestral home when the land they inhabited was designated for white purchase only. They set up a new home in Bumburwi, about twenty-five kilometres away, near the large village of Waddilove in the north-east of the country, where the first African missionary martyr, Bernard Mzeki, was killed. The town of Marandellas has, since independence, been renamed Marondera.

My other great-uncle was the local *n'ganga*, or traditional doctor. His long straight black hair, inherited from an unknown Asian ancestor, made him different in appearance from his younger brother and gave his role as healer and diviner an air of potency. He lived about 150 metres from us and on the same side of the road as we did. The road ran through the village. I sensed as a child that he was held in some awe in the community, and I kept out of his way as much as possible. I only ever visited his homestead with Amai or with my cousin and friend Poona, who was his daughter. On one of those rare visits I recall sitting on Amai's lap as a three-year-old in the dark interior of my great-uncle the n'ganga's kitchen. He wore a headdress which contained feathers and a 'skirt' of feathers and animal bones over his shorts. He was sitting on the floor and dipping a branch into a pot of water which was simmering on the grate – a smooth, round hole in the floor with four large stones around it – and sprinkling the water over the bodies of two children – twins – who were not moving at all. There was an uncertain but not unpleasant aroma emanating from the pot, most probably from the herbs that floated in it. The room was full of people. I clung to my mother because I feared that I too would be sprinkled with boiling water, although it was clear from the stillness of the two little figures that they were not in pain. I was unaware that the twins were dead until Amai explained this to me when, the next day, she went to their funeral. My great-uncle died at an advanced age, estimated by some to have been close to 110 years.

Amai had three houses or adobe rondavels. The biggest and most important house was the kitchen, where most of the living took place. It was a plain room about fifteen feet in diameter with a hearth in the centre. The hearth doubled up as stove, fireplace and even the main source of light on those occasions when Amai had run out of paraffin for the home-made lamp. It consisted of three large rocks placed equidistantly and a fire made in the empty space in the centre. The pots balanced on the corners of the rocks, which could be adjusted to suit the size of the pot. Later she built four clay mounds in place of the stones and fixed the ends of two pieces of iron into the four mounds, so that they crossed each other in the centre. She connected the outer ring of the four mounds with shorter pieces of iron to make a perfect grill, on which it was much easier for the pots to balance.

There were two openings for ventilation on the east and west sides of the wall, close to the thatch. Occasionally a lizard could be seen lounging in the gap, curious beady eyes taking in the peculiar activities of human beings, alert and ready to disappear like a blink into the thatch at the slightest provocation.

The walls in the kitchen were stained black from smoke. When I was about seven years old and on my first visit home from boarding school, I found that I could no longer tolerate it as I must have done before. My eyes burned and I spent my time running in and out of the house or moving from one side of the room to another to escape the smoke, which swirled around before exiting through the gaps in the wall. My brother and my sisters seemed somehow immune. They turned slightly away from the thickest waves but never needed to move away. Built into one side of the wall was a bench where the men sat whenever they were around. Women and children sat on the floor. Apart from my brother Stan, who was only four years older than me, I do not remember any men in our household. However, I have a memory of a time before I started school at the age of four when one evening two white men sat on the bench in the kitchen and ate the traditional staple diet, *sadza*, with us. I never found out who they were and why they were there.

The second house, which stood nearest the road, was the bedroom where Stan and I slept with Amai in the days before I went to school and which doubled as the sitting room when there were special guests. There was a bed and a homemade wooden clothes rack as well as a small table and two chairs. I slept on the floor with Amai and Stan. When my eldest sister Filida bought a proper bed for Amai with her first wages and had it delivered, tied to the roof of the bus, from Marandellas, my mother and I slept on the bed. The bedroom was the same design as the kitchen, minus the hearth, and was the only one of our three houses – as well as the only house in the whole village – to have been whitewashed.

The third house was the storeroom or granary, where

14

Stan slept when he had friends or we had young male extended family members visiting from another village. The granary was where the mealies, the millet, the groundnuts and a variety of other foods were stored. It was also home to mice. Unlike the other two houses, the storeroom was square in order to accommodate the three deep shafts, or storage bins, which were built into one side of the room. It stood on stilts to prevent damp as well as to provide daytime shelter for the chickens. I liked to watch the chickens scrape and scratch the ground under the granary until they each had created a cool hollow into which they sank their bodies, shifting and ruffling their feathers to find the most comfortable position.

The main road was much closer to our side than to the neighbours on the other side. As children we considered ourselves lucky that we did not have to run that far to see who was alighting from the bus; we were always first to help with those precious bags and boxes containing unimaginable treasures from the city.

Behind the row of houses that formed an uneven line along our side of the road was the *vlei*. This was where the village cattle were gathered daily to graze and drink water from the river that flowed, sometimes languidly and sometimes perilously, barely 500 yards from our home but what to a three-year-old had seemed like miles away. The vlei supplied so many of our needs: long, juicy flexible blades of grass for weaving mats and baskets; all manner of wildlife, from grasshoppers to locusts, crickets and mice, which the older children caught and roasted over fires; fat black berries called *hute* that hung from the trees in clusters like grapes; *hacha* or monkey bread , reached by hoisting little ones onto the shoulders of taller boys and girls; or *tsambatsi*, a fruit that grew close to the ground in small clumps and turned black when it was ready for picking. During the rainy season, the vlei would be full of wild cosmos. I often collected bunches of the pretty mauve, pink and white flowers to put into an empty jam jar for my mother. I would run through the cosmos chasing butterflies. Or I and my playmate Poona, who was my age and was one of my herbalist great-uncle's children from his youngest wife, would follow mice trails, crawling silently on our hands and knees, looking like small decapitated heads floating in the long grass, until we found the mouse hole. Then we would sit and wait, believing it to be simply a matter of time before a mouse came out. We never caught any, but even the waiting was fun. Or we would stalk grasshoppers, competing to see who could catch the biggest ones. The clamouring sound of birds was everywhere and every evening there was an orchestral performance by frogs and crickets . . .

I remember a strong sense of community. People gossiped and laughed and called to each other in loud voices as they went past. The village well was close to our homestead. Poona and I enjoyed joining the women when they gathered at the well in the evenings to collect water before the dark settled gently like a wrap around a baby. I remember furtive whisperings followed sometimes by loud guffaws and sharp whacks as the women did high fives to conclude a particularly funny story. Disputes were settled by the village elders and mediated by my uncle, the Headman. I recall *jana*, which was a group of people gathered in the fields or at the home of one family to help with the preparation of the land for tilling or building. They were fed and watered and knew they could arrange a jana for themselves if they needed it. I remember endless blue skies and a climate that kissed you awake in the morning and gently wrapped you up at night. It was a safe, happy childhood.

I spoke no English and have no recollection of being made to feel different. My older sister Margie told me that I was as confident and self-assured as any child surrounded by love. I remember spending a lot of time on my sisters' backs or on the backs of older girls in the village – fetching water from the well, going to the fields, swimming in the river, rambling in the bush in search of wild fruit such as *mazhanje* or picking tsambatsi on the vlei – I was a carefree, happy child. My mother's homestead and the village of which it was a part was my whole world.

One evening I came home from the bush to find Amaiguru Hilda on the bench in the kitchen looking as incongruous as a rabbit in a nest. Amaiguru Hilda and my mother were sisters – *mukoma ne muningina*. Amaiguru Hilda was *mukoma* – the elder sister and Amaiguru to us children – and my mother was *muningina* to her. Amaiguru lived in Marandellas and we all thought that she was smart and sophisticated. She dressed immaculately and wore fashionable hats, which distinguished her from the village women, who wore *doeks* or headscarves. I am not sure if she had ever been to school, but many years later I discovered that she could read and write, possibly learnt when she worked as a matron at Waddilove College. She had an air of authority and when she talked, she made it clear that she would brook no opposition. Her status as the worldly older mother demanded no less than total obedience. Amai, who had never been to school and did not, at that time, read or write, looked up to her, partly because custom expected it, partly because she considered her to be superior to the village women because of her city experience, but also because she feared her sister. We children feared her too. She had a sharp and authoritative voice with which she could flay you like it was a whip if you stepped on the wrong side of her. Amaiguru Hilda never sat on the floor as women were meant to, but on the bench, and even this was only acceptable to her in the absence of a chair. We were captivated by the stories she told about the city; stories of trains so long you could not see where they ended; so many cars that you could not walk in the road and so many white people . . . Something about the mention of white people – *varungu* – sent a frisson of fear through me. But we were curious about their lives and bombarded Amaiguru Hilda with questions.

'What kind of food do the white people eat, Amaiguru?'

'Do they also eat sadza?'

'Where do they cook their food and do they have to go to the bush to find the wood?'

'What do they do the whole day?'

'Do they go to work? What kind of work?'

We learnt that Amaiguru Hilda's employers owned a bottle store – that was their job, and Amaiguru's job was to housekeep for them. Although there was a white family who owned and lived on the tobacco farm on the other side of the river and whose lands stretched all the way to Waddilove, and although it seemed to me like the whole village worked there when it was tobacco-picking season, it was hard to imagine what work the white people actually did.

My heart skipped when Amaiguru said, 'Would you like to come with me to Salisbury tomorrow, Maudie? Then you can see the city yourself and I can show you the train and buy you some nice new clothes.'

I looked at Stan, my eyes and my mouth wide open and said, 'Can Stennie come too?'

'No,' Amaiguru said, 'I can only take one person. He can come next time.'

The excitement gave way to anxiety and I had to ask, 'Do white people really turn naughty children into corned beef?'

Amaiguru laughed. 'Of course not. That's just a game you village children play.'

I was never sure about Amaiguru's response and was

inclined to believe the factory story. How could it not be true when children spoke with such authority about the tip of a finger in a corned-beef tin? I listened to these stories about the wondrous world in which Amaiguru Hilda lived, unable to contain my excitement about visiting the big city at last.

I was blissfully unaware that my life was about to change for ever.

Many years later, when Amiguru Hilda came to visit me in England, we had detailed discussions about the circumstances of my being sent away to school. I was particularly curious about what my mother felt about me being sent so far away. Much of what I have written here is what I imagine that I, as a four-year-old, would have thought and felt listening to their conversation.

It was night-time. I lay in the bed I shared with my mother but which on that night I would share with Amaiguru. Although it was a single bed, it took up most of the space in our small round bedroom. Amai and Amaiguru Hilda were sitting at the small table that stood to the right of the entrance. The table and two chairs, made by someone in the village, were the only other furniture in the room. There was a lamp in the centre of the table made from an empty jam jar that contained paraffin. A twisted piece of cloth, coiled like a snake, lay soaking in the paraffin while its end piece, which was lit, was pulled through a small hole in the lid, looking like a reticent cobra wondering whether or not to strike. The smell of paraffin and burning cloth was strong, but I was used to it. Usually the dogs from the other side of the village made a lot of noise in the night, and when they started barking, the dogs from our side also joined in to form a discordant barking choir. But that night they were quiet. Amaiguru and Amai's voices were a low rumble, Amaiguru's voice sounding like Danger, our dog, growling. Ever inquisitive about the mysterious world of grown-ups, my ears, sharp as a puppy's, were honed to the sound of their voices.

I closed my eyes and pretended to be asleep.

'You know she can't go to the local school,' Amaiguru Hilda stressed. 'She has to go to a school for children of her kind. If you keep her, she'll never have an education. Is that what you want for her? When she grows up, she will never forgive you.'

'It's not that,' Amai lamented. 'It's the fact that she can't come home for such a long time and won't be able to spend all her holidays with us here.'

'Well, that's just how it is. The law forbids her to attend a school for African children, so you have no choice. You have to send her to school. You should consider yourself lucky that the government will pay for her education.'

'Eee, it's hard, Mukoma – to be given such a choice! She is going so far away. What if she forgets us? How will I ever afford the train fare to go all the way to Bulawayo? I don't even have the money to send Margie and Abigail to school. I should at least take her to the train myself.'

'Be sensible, Serina. That will just make it harder for both of you. Best say your goodbyes here. Haven't you got other children to worry about, and am I not her mother too?'

I did not understand what, or who, they were talking about. But it could not be me. I was an African child and I would be going to school with my brother Stan. I opened my eyes and sat up. Amai was crying.

'What are you talking about, Amai?'

'Oh, it's just grown-up talk,' Amaiguru snapped. 'Go to sleep, otherwise you will be too tired to go to Salisbury tomorrow.'

I lay there wondering if I should go to Salisbury after all. I did not want to see my Amai crying. I felt a pain in my throat as I struggled not to cry. I wanted to get out of bed and sit on Amai's lap and make her feel better, but I was afraid that Amaiguru would change her mind and not take me with her, and I desperately wanted to visit the city. There would be so much to tell Stan and all my friends in the village when I returned. I turned my thoughts to the fun Stan and I had had that morning as we chased the chicken that Amai wanted to cook in honour of Amaiguru. I fell asleep thinking about the unlucky chicken who – after my sister Margie had chopped its head off in one clean swipe – stood up, headless, and ran around in a circle, finally flopping lifeless to the ground.

Three

I was five years old and sitting with other children on the floor in Sub A, the reception classroom at Sacred Heart Home. Rows of small desks filled the room behind us. There were pictures, whose nature I cannot recall, stuck on the walls in every direction. We were learning phonetics and repeating the sounds Sister Dagoberta called out. Sister Dagoberta sat on a chair in front of us and held up large cards with letters on them.

'A-A-A-A,' she said, sounding like a sheep.

'A-A-A-A,' we repeated.

'B-B-B-B.' She puffed out the letter and we copied her.

The shutters of my memory open clearly on this lesson. In my mind the faces of the other children are indistinct yet strangely familiar. In that early memory, I see Sister Dagoberta as a large woman, swathed from head to foot in what I now know is a nun's habit. I cannot make out the details of her face. But I think it is kind. I am no longer afraid of her or any of the nuns, and their clothes no longer strike me as strange. As I sit in front of Sister Dagoberta, I focus on the large cross hanging from a red ribbon around her neck. It had fascinated me from the first time I saw it, this naked man with nothing but a loincloth, suspended from the cross, looking sad, asleep or dead – certainly not happy. I would soon be drawn into the beliefs and rituals that surrounded him and that guided the whole of my school years. For the time being, I am curious about everything. At some indefinable point in the last year, I had adjusted to my new circumstances, losing my fear of white people and learning to trust the nuns. The English language crept up on me surreptitiously, as the alphabet in that reception class is the first time I remember speaking since I asked for my cow in chiZezuru a year earlier. I am settling in, speaking only English because we were discouraged from speaking our mother tongues. I cannot remember how much English I was able to speak at this stage.

Try as I might to prise them open, the shutters remain closed to everything that happened between my falling asleep on the train and the lesson with Sister Dagoberta. I do not remember the train arriving in Bulawayo; I do not remember travelling to the school or with whom; I remember nothing at all of that first year – it is a dark tunnel.

Our school, Sacred Heart Home, was established as a home for Coloured children. It was founded in 1946 by two missionary sisters of the Precious Blood, Sister Aquilina and Sister Didyma. It is said that the land belonged to the big-game hunter Courtney Selous, and although a working farm, was bought by Cecil John Rhodes for the Precious Blood sisters to establish an educational facility for the growing number of Coloured children in the country. Coloureds were the descendants or the children of a mixed heritage. This could be one of many descriptions. The most common in Rhodesia were the offspring and descendants of an African and a European, usually a white man with a black woman. It was rare during my childhood to find someone who was the child of a black man and a white woman, and the anti-miscegenation laws, which could see a black man killed for the offence of sex with a white woman, helped to keep those figures low. I knew of only one child of this background throughout my childhood and up to the time I left the country. Other Coloured mixtures included South Asian, Chinese or Arab with African – again, this was commonly men with African or Coloured women. This designation of Coloured as someone who had mixed heritage was unique to South Africa and Rhodesia. Here it does not refer to Africans, as it did in the United States, or to anyone who was not white, as it did in the United Kingdom.

The school was a short distance as the crow flies from a railway siding called Bushtick, which served an old gold mine, and perhaps because Sacred Heart Home was a small mouthful, the school became popularly known as Bushtick. Before Sacred Heart Home, most Coloured children of my mother's and my generation who lived in the villages did not go to school.

From the earliest days of Rhodesian colonialism, the education of African and Coloured children had been largely left to missionaries. You were therefore fortunate if your family lived in a village within a reasonable distance of a mission school. Government primary schools in the rural areas were later built, but were initially few and far between. In the 1950s, because of segregation laws, these schools were not meant for Coloured children. Embakwe, located in the south of the country and founded in 1921, and St John's in the capital Salisbury, founded in 1924, were the first missionary schools for Coloured children. They were established on the belief that these children should be removed from the rural African environment and, because their fathers were white, should be assimilated into a European culture. All the schools for Coloured children were co-educational.

Categorised as 'European' in the Education Act of 1930 – which made education compulsory for Europeans – but unable to attend European or African schools because of the policy of separation of the races, Coloured children, especially in rural areas, had nowhere to go other than to the cities, where the few government primary schools set aside for them were already overcrowded. Finally, responding to pressure from missionaries and from members of the Coloured communities in the towns, a commission of inquiry was set up to look into the condition of Coloured children living in the rural areas. The subsequent Education Act of 1938 made education compulsory for Coloured children – as it was for white children – but this resulted in even more pressure on existing schools, as government negligence had meant that there were not enough spaces to meet the demand. During the late 1940s and into the 1950s, attempts by middle-class Coloured families who could afford to pay to send their children to schools for whites were often strongly resisted by white parents keen to preserve the colour bar. Missionaries were the ones who stepped in, and Sacred Heart Home in Matabeleland, and Martindale in Mashonaland, both offering boarding facilities, made it possible for Coloured children from far and wide to at least have a primary education. There were only two government secondary schools for Coloured students – Founders High School, in Bulawayo, the first government secondary school for Coloureds (1952), and Morgan High School in Salisbury (1956). The government had to rent hostels in Bulawayo for students who attended Founders High and had to build a hostel for those who attended Morgan High School but did not live in the city of Salisbury.

I had a friend called Pat. She was a few months older than me, with large, wide-spaced, intelligent eyes, a nose that curled slightly upwards and a pretty button mouth. Like mine, her hair was short and frizzy, parted down the centre, with two short plaits on either side of her head. Although our 'carers', older girls allotted with this charge, took responsibility for keeping our hair neat and tidy, the girls in the school acquired the art of plaiting each other's, if not their own, hair almost as soon as they attained the age of five.

Pat was from Bulawayo and could speak Sindebele, the language of the people who were descendants of the Zulus who had migrated north from South Africa. She told me captivating stories about her family. Her home sounded so different from mine, so 'European'. I had never been to the house of the white farming family where my mother and others in the village went to work during the tobacco-picking season. It was hard to imagine rooms in an ordinary house that were so big that they could hold two beds in them, especially if the kitchen and bathroom were also under the same roof.

Pat's parents were Coloured, a term that at age five I was still unaware applied to me. I learnt much later that both Pat's grandmothers were black and her grandfathers were white. But I knew nothing about the complexities or political implications of race. Pat's father worked on the railways. That, I learnt much later, was one of the jobs allocated to or reserved for Coloured men. I had a mother whom I had not seen in a year and, despite Pat's stories, I do not recall questioning, at that age, the absence of a father in my own life.

The bell was ringing. Pat put ribbons at the end of my plaits and stood back to admire her handiwork. My plaits were sticking out sideways like they were about to take off, so she pulled hard on them to keep them pointing straight down. It was time for supper. We lined up in twos near the lemon hedge, youngest in the front, oldest children at the back, and walked down the slope to the dining room, where the boys were already waiting for the doors to open. The sun was setting, sending a reddish-orange glow across the horizon. It would be almost dark by the time we left and went back to the boarding areas.

We sat on benches at long rectangular tables, the girls on one side of the dining room and the boys on the other. There was a crucifix hanging on one wall, and on the opposite wall a picture of Mary holding the baby Jesus with halos suspended behind their heads. Mary was presented as a white woman and was dressed in red with a blue cloak. She was not cuddling her baby and her gaze was outwards, looking down at us with love – or was it pity? Baby Jesus, naked, with rolls of fat around his chubby waist, sat stiffly, balanced on his mother's hand. Someone had put the caption 'Baby Jesus Meek and Mild' below the picture to remind us how to behave. I sat next to Pat.

'That boy likes you,' she said, nodding her head in the direction of one of the boys within our vision. We giggled. Pat enjoyed teasing me.

'Shh, Patricia, no talking,' said the nun in charge, and we looked at each other and giggled again. The nun came and, taking Pat by the hand, she moved her to another table. It was Friday, so we were having fish for dinner. I did not particularly like the food but I did not have a problem eating it. On the other hand, Angela, who had replaced Pat next to me, had problems with all her meals. She would sit staring at her plate, frowning, until one of the maids would come and start forking the food into her mouth while she grimaced, chewing with difficulty. She had particular problems with porridge in the mornings. We all had problems with the mealie-meal porridge, which sometimes had weevils in it, but while the rest of us had learnt to close our eyes and eat whatever was placed in front of us because the nuns always reminded us to learn from Jesus, Angela would clench her teeth when someone tried to feed her. Day after day she was made to sit there until she had eaten all her porridge. One day we came back to the dining room for a mid-morning snack only to find Angela still sitting at the table, the porridge on her plate looking like something the cat vomited. She had been left there to finish her porridge and then forgotten.

After supper we walked back to our boarding areas in the fading light and to the sound of evensong coming from the church, and we played in the quadrangle before bedtime. The dormitory was shaped like a barn, large and rectangular with a zinc roof. When it rained the noise was like a jet flying low, so that we could shout as loudly as we wanted and we would still have difficulty hearing each other. We were like little wild animals released from a cage when we gathered in the dormitory during the rain. All the hours of silence and good behaviour disappeared as we ran among the beds chasing each other and screaming with delight until Sister came around with a stick and made us all sit quietly on the floor at the front end of the dormitory. Tamed, we would sit patiently until we were told to collect books, games and puzzles, and we would entertain ourselves soberly until the rain stopped or it was time for bed.

The dormitory had high ceilings with large windows, which had ropes that you pulled to open and shut them. It had tall pillars that divided the room in two along its length. There was a commode at the bottom, near the entrance to the room of the nun in charge. The older girls, nine to thirteen years or maybe older, occupied the top half of the room and the younger, five-to-eight-year-olds, or 'babies', were at the bottom end of the room, near the commode. Pat and I were on the babies' side. At night, when there was complete silence in the dormitory, we could sometimes hear hyenas calling and laughing in the distance and 'did you hear that? did you hear that?' whispered like wind in long grass through the beds. We ducked our heads under the covers and waited for sleep to come.

The heat before the rain felt thick and heavy. The dormitory was an oven. As soon as the lights were turned off, I whispered to Pat, 'It's so hot. Let's sleep on the floor.' We crawled under our beds to lie on the cool concrete floor and giggled because we found it daring. But Sister Dagoberta, who was known to walk around at night tucking children in and placing sweets under the pillows of children who had behaved themselves during the day, found us fast asleep under our beds. She thought me too timid to come up with something naughty, so the next day she told Pat, 'You must not lead others into temptation,' and moved her to a bed in the next row from me.

Four

Pat and I were lingering near the fence, which was the
boundary of the girls' boarding area. Behind the fence
was strictly out of bounds. We were standing in the far
corner, where there was a tall marula tree with logs beneath
it for us to sit on and a small tin shed with bits of orange peel
scattered and left by us children to dry, like mopane worms,
on the roof. We often played at doctors or teachers here with
other children, pretending that the little shed was a hospital
or a school office, where we doled out dried orange peel for
medicine or reward.

That day Pat and I stood holding onto the fence and looking onto the scrub, which spread all the way to St Joseph's
Hill, where we were sometimes taken for walks and allowed
to run wild among the trees. We stared into the shimmering
heat and tried to spot bees or butterflies flitting between the
low bushes in the dry, sparse scrubland. I was staring at a
large locust with one leg, hopping lopsidedly.

'Look,' Pat said, pointing.

'It's got only one leg,' I said, nodding wisely.

'Um-hm,' she responded.

She stared at it, deep in thought, then asked, 'Why do locus always have only one leg?'

'No, they don't.'

'Yes, they do. That one's got.'

'Well, that one's only one, isn't it?'

'No, it's not. I always seen them with one leg. I think a snake eated the other one.'

'It didunt. If a snake wants to eat a locus leg, it would eat both of them, isn't it.'

'Well, maybe the locus hopped away when it felt the snake biting its leg.'

'No it didunt. A snake is so fast it would just stick out its tongue and eat the whole locus.'

'Well, why does that one have only one leg then?'

'I don't know. Maybe a scorpion bited it.'

'No it didunt.'

'Well, I said maybe.'

'No, it can't, because a scorpion bites with its tail. When my mummy found a scorpion in our cupboard, she told the "boy" to kill it and he told me that it can bite you with its tail.'

'Does it have teeth in its tail, then?'

'Yah, because otherwise it can't bite, isn't it. It bites with its tail first, then it puts the locus in its mouth.'

'It's got teeth in its mouth orso?'

Pat looked at me thoughtfully and then shrugged.

'Well, I dunno!' she said, defeated.

'Shame, poor locus,' I said, my heart aching with pity. After a short pause, I said, 'I seen lots of lizards with no tail.'

'Even me, I seen them.'

'Did the scorpion eat the tails?'

'Uh-huh, but it growed back.'

We stood quietly thinking our separate thoughts, me about the remarkable lives of locusts and scorpions, when an

African man walked by along the little path that piggy-backed the school fence. He was wearing flannel trousers that had been cut at the knees and a short-sleeved khaki shirt, and was barefoot. He carried a hoe over his shoulder. There was something so familiar about this that I gripped the fence more tightly and stared at the man as he went by, whistling and not looking at us. The only African man I had noticed in my time in the school before this was the driver. He wore a well-starched khaki safari suit and a cap, and I had only ever seen him getting in or out of the school van or 'combi', and then usually from a distance. African men at the school mainly worked in the fields. Suddenly Pat took off, shouting, 'Run, Maudie, run!'

'Why?' I asked, puzzled.

'There's a man. Run!'

'Where?' I asked, turning around and running towards the dormitory buildings after her.

'That man there. If Sister sees you talking to him, you'll get in trouble.'

'But I wasn't,' I said, puffing and panting in my effort to catch up with her.

'Yes, but when you see them, you must run away. They could steal you and turn your bones into *muti*.'

We were breathing heavily as we walked over to our favourite spot near the mulberry trees and sat down with some other children. Pat began telling stories about the wicked activities of witch doctors, who bought bones and other body parts from black men who pounced on children and killed them. The witch doctors then used the children's bodies for medicine which we called muti. I listened to her, spellbound. A little group formed and suddenly the air was thick with tales of witch doctors and the dangers that black people in general posed to innocent little Coloured girls. 'They even can eat you and drink your blood,' one girl said,

33

and as if it was too much to bear, the crowd began to disperse. Pat changed the subject and started talking about her little brother. But I was no longer listening to Pat because I was drawing in the dust and thinking about what had just happened. Her voice sounded as if it was coming from the other side of the playground.

Exasperated, she said, 'Maud, you're not listening.'

'I am,' I lied.

I tried to concentrate on Pat, but that lasted only a few minutes. I was lost in my own thoughts about the man, sure that he would arrive at a field of maize and would spend the day hoeing, sweat pouring down his dark face, and singing a song that was familiar to me. In the evening he would go home to his family and sit on a bench carved into the wall of his house, which would be round. Someone, a girl, would bring him a dish so that he could wash his hands and eat the food that was placed in front of him.

But here, he was a dark and evil presence ready to hurt little Coloured girls, to sell them to a witch doctor who would turn their bones into *muti*.

Pat's voice interrupted my reverie. She sounded cross. She stood up and walked away, saying, 'Well, if you don't want to hear my stories, I'm going.'

I watched Pat leave but, as if my bones had already been taken from me, I flopped forward like a deflated balloon, and ran my hands through the sand, which neither yielded any answers nor helped me make sense of the things I had heard.

In the new world I had entered, Black African men were called 'boys' and their job was to work in the gardens and the fields. When they were not working they were 'men', something to be afraid of. I was learning from Pat and the other children that there was no end to their bad ways. We were to keep as far away from them as possible.

In the village these same people were my loving brothers and cousins, uncles and generous friends – people I trusted. I did not know what a witch doctor was and did not realise that the term was being used to describe traditional doctors like my great-uncle the n'ganga, whose instincts and knowledge of herbs were relied on completely by the people in the village and for miles around. Although he had power in the village, I knew him as a healer, not a killer. As for my uncle Marondera, with his gentle eyes, his teasing smile, his willingness to help all who came to him, he was not compatible with the image that struck such fear in the hearts and minds of the children at school. African women, known to me in another world as caring mothers, sisters, cousins, aunts, were here called 'nannies' and their role was to clean and look after us. So what did that make my mother? I was so confused.

At age five, I had no idea what backgrounds the other children came from. I did not know that I was a Coloured or what that meant. I could only think of what I had experienced and was utterly confused by it, as it contradicted everything I knew about my family, who looked like the man we had seen and like the women who looked after us. No doubt there were some children raised in rural areas who were learning, like me, about the different categories in our society and realising that there was a hierarchy in place. Our understanding of these issues differed depending on whether we lived in rural areas, where one hardly saw white people and certainly had no concept of nannies, or in the cities, where different 'races' and their roles in society were taken for granted. Then one day I happened to be talking to Julia, a girl only a year or two older than me but physically much bigger, who had decided to be my friend and protector. I was a skinny child but I had never been singled out for bullying. I was surprised when Julia said, 'If anyone does anything to you, you can come and tell me, OK?'

'OK,' I said, while I searched my memory for anyone who had wronged me so that I could tell Julia and show my trust and gratitude. I found no one. But something else was troubling me a great deal. At first I hesitated, then said, 'You know the nannies?'

'Yah', she said.

I paused for a while, uncertain and unsafe with the subject I was raising.

'Well, my mummy looks like that,' I mumbled, looking away and across the playground trying to appear indifferent.

'My mummy also,' Julia said. I felt a surge of relief and courage. I wasn't the only one! But I didn't dare ask if her mother lived in a house like my mother's. I wanted to be like Pat, with a daddy who worked on the railways, a mummy who was not a nanny, and a family who lived in a nice house. I didn't want to live in the village anymore, in huts, and I didn't want my friends to know that my family lived in them still. I was, at that time, oblivious of the struggles of many Coloured people – the overcrowding in many homes and the fight for more and better housing than the government was providing. Coloured people had been lobbying the government for many years and the government had turned a deaf ear. Although the situation had eased a little in the 1950s – largely due to the existence, between 1953 and 1963, of the Federation of Rhodesia and Nyasaland – poorer members of the Coloured community continued to face pressure over housing, especially as more Coloureds were leaving the rural areas to seek work in the towns.

A house that contained two bedrooms was to my mind a luxurious house. I had no idea that my mother's accommodation was traditional to that part of the world and was adequate living space, certainly more than in some of the overcrowded homes provided for Coloured people by the government. In response to Pat's accounts of her family,

I started making up stories about a lovely home with a Coloured sister and little brother, and about cousins who lived in Salisbury. A part of me was glad that my mother had not come to see me, because then everyone would know where I came from. But now I was not alone. Julia – and who knew who else – was in the same situation that I was in. We were all being gradually moulded into a way of thinking that would alienate many Coloured families from their African relatives. I just could not ask Julia about what kind of home she had because that would involve me talking about my own home.

'So, does it mean I'm a nanny?' I asked Julia.

'No, coz your daddy is a European, isn't it?'

I felt as though something large and heavy had been thrown at me and hit me straight between my eyes. I ruminated, turning her words this way and that to understand their meaning. The words merely shouted and hammered inside my brain. *'Your daddy'! What was she talking about? How could this be? How did she know? Surely if I had had a daddy at all, I would have seen him or my mother would have said something?*

Julia talked about a European father as if it was something to be proud of. If that was the case, why had no one ever said anything to me about him? And where was he? Julia lived in Salisbury and seemed more worldly, so I trusted her knowledge. On one level I was relieved that my father was a European because, naturally, he would have a European house. I wondered if the nuns knew him. Would I be allowed to stay with him and have my own bedroom? I began to imagine what my bedroom would look like, though I could not go beyond Pat's description of a bed and toys. Would I share the bedroom with other children? Who were they and what would they be like? Would they be Europeans like him? While it was a pleasant daydream, the information also felt like a burden that I would have to carry – at least, until my mother resolved it for me. And at that early stage in my school life, it seemed to me unlikely that I would ever see my mother again.

Five

It was a few days before the Christmas school holidays in December 1957. I was seven years old. Sister Dagoberta accosted me in the playground.

'Would you like to go home for Christmas this year?'

She might just as well have asked if I wanted to go to England – some vague place out there where Europeans came from and nothing I could do would conjure an image of where it was or what would happen there. My answer was an automatic, 'Yes, Sister.' I was not even sure if I did want to go 'home'. I had not seen my mother in three years. I had adjusted to the idea that I was one of the orphans who had no home to go to. I had only truly felt the sadness of my situation when the holidays arrived and the hollow silence around the school would seem to enter my being, leaving me bereft and abandoned.

Although I was one of a few children who stayed at school during holidays, my closest friends had left and so the first week of the holidays was a time of loneliness and grief that I found difficult to shake off. I would wander forlornly to the furthest extremities of the school boundaries and sit and stare out towards St Joseph's Hill on one side or Falcon College, a private school for white boys, which could only just be seen in the distance, or I would take my book and sit under the mulberry trees and read or reread Enid Blyton. At seven I was obsessed with the Secret Seven stories, and later the Famous Five and Malory Towers series, my enjoyment of these books a testament to the extent to which I assimilated a section of British culture.

'Well, your mother has asked for you to come,' Sister Dagoberta said. 'You can go on the train with the others to Salisbury and your mother will meet you at the station.' I saw Florrie, one of the girls that also stayed at school during the holidays, standing near the concrete sink at the corner of the dormitory building and ran to her.

'I'm going home. Sister told me just now', I blurted out, jumping up and down and trying hard to sound enthusiastic. What I really wanted was to gauge someone else's response to this idea of going home – someone who, like me, considered the school her home.

'You lucky,' Florrie said, looking at me with hollow dark eyes. 'I'm not going.'

'My mummy is going to meet me at the station in Salisbury,' I continued with exaggerated enthusiasm, oblivious to how she must have been feeling about my show of excitement. Something about the mention of Salisbury station made me pause. I found it difficult to imagine what that meant – Salisbury station. I was filled with doubt and a small niggling fear, and I wanted badly for someone to reassure me that going home was the best thing that could happen to me.

'Will there be lots of people in the station?' I wanted to know.

'Yah, there's always lots of people coz it's such a big station.'

'So how will I find my mummy?'

40

'I don't know. Maybe Sister will help you.'

I stayed the rest of the day with Florrie, absorbing her sadness as well as her safety. I did not want to imagine what lay beyond the school boundaries.

I clung to Louisa, who was eight, a year older than me, and who I sometimes played with. This was my first sighting of a train at close hand since that fateful journey when I was four years old. We had occasionally seen a train in the distance, passing through Bushtick Siding, puffing smoke and emitting its evocative whistle – a rare sight for us as we stood on St Joseph's Hill. I followed Louisa onto the train and we searched for our names on the wall near the door of the compartment. Louisa was excited to show me how everything worked. With an 'isn't it perfect?' expression on her face, she pointed to what looked like a wooden panel between two windows on the wall and directly above a little metal sink.

'That's a table', she said conspiratorially. 'They going to bring it down tomorrow for our breakfast.' Nothing in my imagination could conjure up how this wooden panel stuck upright on the wall and tucked in between the windows could be used as a table until the older girls sharing our compartment demonstrated.

'Guess where we sleep?' Louisa challenged, wide-eyed.

'On the seats?' I asked bouncing on my bottom to test if one could really sleep on the hard, upholstered seat.

'Yah, but there are four beds – two here,' she said, sitting on one seat, 'and two here,' her hands waving dramatically at the seat on the other side of the compartment and clearly enjoying the mystified look on my face. I could only see two seats, so she pointed to the backrest. Breathing heavily and grunting, she tried to put the backrest to its bed position, but managed to pull it just far enough for me to see its double function. 'See?' She nodded triumphantly and with obvious relief, letting it fall back into place.

'Someone will come to put it up and make the beds,' she added, in case I should worry about having to face the mammoth task myself.

Older now, and not as frightened as I had been three years earlier, I was experiencing a train properly for the first time. I thought it was one of the most beautiful things I had ever seen, with its dark, shining, polished wood, the windows with the RR insignia, the two Rs overlapping like lovers in an embrace. I traced my finger over the letters to feel the grain, wondering how they had managed to etch the letters onto the glass without breaking it. I was enthralled by everything and sat by the open window staring at a goods train idling on the next line. Louisa and I ran into the corridor to stand by the windows and watch people come and go until we were told to go back into our compartment for a final headcount.

Then the train let out a piercing whistle. A smell of sulphur wafted through the air. The train gave a jerk, startling me as it lurched forward. With my fingers clenched and eyebrows bowing to each other, I looked at Louisa, who stared out of the window unperturbed. The people on the platform seemed to be gliding slowly away from us; soon they were out of sight and we were speeding through the darkness and out through open savannah.

Louisa was shaking me.

'Get up. We are nearly in Salisbury. Sister Dominic says we have to wash and have our breakfast.'

'Have we passed Kwee Kwee already?'

The older girls who had slept on the top bunks laughed loudly.

'It's not Kwee Kwee. It's Kway Kway. Anyway, we reached Que Que during the night when you were sleeping,' said one

42

of them, keen to demonstrate that, as an 'older' girl, she did not sleep on the journey.

I felt embarrassed to have said something stupid, but I was also deeply disappointed. Louisa and I had wanted to be awake to see the steam train taking in water, which we had been told happened in the town of Que Que.

We took it in turns at the little sink. A black man in a starched uniform walked in and tidied up the sink and then unlocked the wooden panel above and lowered it over the sink. Two panels were connected to the sides of the central wooden beam and they were unfolded, which immediately trebled the width of the table. I felt nervous about the black man and looked at Louisa. She had seen it all before. The other two girls seemed equally unconcerned to have a black man with us in the narrow confines of the compartment. The man removed the bedding, placed it in a large bag and then tucked the top bunks away so that we could sit comfortably. We were ready for breakfast.

Salisbury station was buzzing with activity.

Several heads popped out of the train windows and called to their families waiting for them as the train slowed down to a halt. I descended onto the platform with Louisa, who had seen her mother. I was surprised to see that Louisa's mother was not a Coloured but was black, just like my mother.

'Is your mummy here?' Louisa asked.

'I don't know. I can't see her,' I replied, wondering if I would recognise my mother.

Sister Dominic came over to talk to Louisa's mother. I had to say goodbye to my friend. I looked at Sister Dominic. What if no one were to come and collect me? What would happen to me? Sister Dominic took my hand and walked around with me as she saw the other children off with their respective families.

Time seemed to drag, but the buzz of the station gradually died down.

Salisbury station did not seem half as big as on that first visit with Aunt Hilda, and although there were lots of people, it did not seem as noisy either. It was of course daytime, as opposed to the night of my first visit, so I was not as distracted by the lights. Nevertheless, the station fascinated me just as much. There was more colour, and not just in the clothes people wore, but in the posters, the colour of the building, the many porters in their uniforms trundling back and forth with their trolleys. I was not afraid but interested, albeit with just a bit more sophistication. Yet a little worm of anxiety nibbled at me. Time was passing, the station was emptying of passengers, and I was still there. Sister Dominic was talking to someone in an office. Then I was asked to sit down on my suitcase near the station-master's office and a man with a camera started taking pictures of me. Sister Dominic's kind eyes looked into my anxious ones.

'Well, Maud, we shall have to take you with us to the Convent, and if no one claims you by the time we have to go back to Bulawayo tomorrow night, you will have to return to school with us.'

The shame of having to go back to the school and explain it to those who, like me, never went anywhere was unbearable to think about. What had happened to my mother? Had she died? Was I now properly one of the orphans?

Sister took my hand and followed a man to a waiting car.

The following morning she showed me the newspaper.

'Let's hope that now you are famous, someone will recognise you and come for you,' she said. A picture of a forlorn little girl sitting on a suitcase near the station-master's office was plastered on the front page of the *Rhodesia Herald*: 'Child Abandoned at Railway Station' said the headline.

Six

Amaiguru Hilda and I were back at the railway station in Salisbury boarding the train for Marandellas. I looked around me and wondered if my aunt had made a mistake. This was not the same as the grand carriage I had travelled in from Bulawayo to Salisbury. Instead of a compartment with upholstered seats, sinks, and tables that could miraculously disappear, we were in a large open carriage. There were wooden benches with slats in rows facing each other with a corridor running through the centre of the carriage and wooden racks above the seats spanning its length. The racks were bursting with luggage of every variety, from suitcases to cardboard boxes and baskets. Every space on the benches was occupied. Some women had babies still tied to their backs; others had babies clinging to their breasts; there were old men, felt hats balancing on their heads, leaning on knobkerries – hunting canes also used for walking – and old women with colourful doeks tied around their heads; there were children sitting quietly staring (some of them at me); there were younger men in suits, and women like Amaiguru Hilda in dresses pressed to perfection – everyone seemed to be in their Sunday best. I still wore my school uniform. I felt certain that this carriage must be temporary and that soon we would be transported to the grander style of compartment that I had travelled on only the day before. This did not happen. I soon realised that Amaiguru had not made a mistake. This was the third-class carriage for Africans. I was the only Coloured person present.

With a hiss and a loud whistle, the train moved, hauling itself reluctantly and heavily like a garden slug, iron wheels screeching as if being tortured. Slowly the city disappeared and we were in the suburbs with their neat pavements; their pretty white houses with red-, blue- or green-tiled roofs like colourful umbrellas neatly spaced apart; their large gardens fastidiously laid out and separated from their neighbours' by tidy hedges or trees flowering flamboyantly; their gates with signs that said '*Chenjera imbwa*!' (Beware of the dog).

From the distance we spied Tafara township, where the black people lived. Here the small, whitewashed houses were crowded together and surrounded by maize or sheltered from their neighbours by mango trees. We shunted through Epworth, a moonlike landscape of gigantic igneous boulders strewn randomly by the large hand of the Ice Age, some of them seeming to balance precariously yet solidly grounded. Finally, we were in open farmland with tall eucalyptus trees concealing the farmhouses from the gaze of passing travellers. The train passed small railway sidings like Ruwa, Bromley and Melfort, and stopped for water once. Without friends with whom to comment and share the mysterious workings of the steam train, I stayed in my seat and paid little attention to what was going on outside. The journey was slow and tedious for me but the other passengers, including Amaiguru Hilda, exchanged news and views as if they had always known each other.

I did not speak at all during the journey except to say yes

or no to the occasional question asked by Amaiguru Hilda. I looked out at the *musasa* trees staining the land sienna, orange and burnished gold as far as the eye could see. I followed bush paths of smooth white sand as they criss-crossed each other and disappeared into the thickets beyond. The houses were more difficult to see, hidden by trees and camouflaged by the leaves. I experienced a jolt of delight when I did see some, the unpredictability of spotting life when I had decided that the paths were endless, going on into boundless countryside and who knew where else. Importantly, and with mixed feelings, I saw that they were the same type of houses as those my mother lived in. I caught the eyes of little boys and girls who appeared suddenly, like curious creatures of the wild, barefoot, one or two in ragged clothes, to stand and stare at the passing train.

Then neat little European-style houses appeared, which, though small, looked well cared for, with gardeners occasionally visible: trimming, cutting, sweeping. These must be the houses of white people. I learnt later that these were indeed retirement homes for white people. The train gradually slowed down, and with a hiss and a slight jerk, it sidled into the station at Marandellas.

I stood on the platform and watched people erupting like a multicoloured army of ants from the train with their suitcases and their mysterious bundles, and listened to the dissonant sounds coming from every direction. Amaiguru Hilda was sorting out our luggage, shuffling it around like pieces of a jigsaw as she worked out how to manage my suitcase, her large shopping bag, her handbag and possibly me, as it was quite a long walk for a child from the station to her house in the township. While I waited for her, my attention had been drawn to a gigantic billboard, which I was staring at and trying to make sense of. The billboard had a boy of about ten years old chasing after a chicken and pouring salt

47

on its back. There was a caption in large letters which said, 'See how it runs!' Why was the boy wasting salt by pouring it on the chicken's back? Surely all one had to do was chase the chicken and it would run. I was still puzzling over the billboard when Amaiguru called to me to follow her. She had her shopping bag in one hand and was clutching her hand-bag in the other while the suitcase balanced neatly unaided on her head, as if it were a grotesque alien extension that had suddenly sprung up there. Despite her bags, she walked steadily to the front of the train and with many other people we waded across the railway line – the only means of cross-ing to the other side.

It was a long walk to her house in aptly named Dombo-tombo, 'The Rocks', but I was relieved to be moving my limbs after the train journey. I kicked the dust on the road, spraying my school shoes with a fine brown powder, jumped on the large stones that scabbed the ground, protruding like warts in the road. I had to run to catch up with my aunt.

There was a group of children playing on the road. They stopped and stared at me. Then, as if suddenly realising that the circus had come into town, they started running alongside us, shouting, '*Murungu dhunu, murungu dhunu.*' Puzzled that they should be mistaking me for an albino, I stared back. They continued chanting, running to keep up with us, laughing and occasionally somersaulting in our path, legs grey with dust. I soon realised that they were not greeting me or trying to be friendly. They were making fun of me. My face burned with embarrassment and I stuck as closely as I could to Amaiguru Hilda.

'Get lost,' Amaiguru chided, putting the bags down, probably to take a much-needed rest but pretending to look for a stick. The children scattered, shouting, '*Wona murungu dhunu,*' pointing at me as they encouraged each other and laughed.

48

Finally we arrived in front of a row of little houses painted white with small front yards, some of which were strewn with large rocks, just as the name of the township suggested. Curious people stood in their yards and on the dusty road and stared. A young boy emerged from one of the houses and ran towards us, his face beaming. His hair was cut close to the scalp, accentuating his small eyes and slightly protruding ears. He hugged me tightly and lifted me off my feet, saying, 'Hello, Maudie.' I did not recognise him right away and, averting my eyes, I whispered timidly, 'Hello.'

'Aaah, but you don't know me?' he said in English, in a tone which suggested that we had met only the other day. He bent his head to look into my face. Gradually it dawned on me – my brother and former best friend, Stan. I had not, in three years, communicated with any member of my family. At school we were taught to write letters to our parents – simple childish tracts that said, 'Dear Mummy. How are you? I am fine. I like school. Your loving daughter, Maud,' and which were probably never sent. The school would have had Amaiguru Hilda's address, but would they have sent my letter and those of all the other children at the school's expense? I had no idea.

'Stennie,' I said flatly. I looked at him and smiled, but I was not sure what to do or how to behave. Stan was now eleven years old and towered over me. He laughed loudly and said, 'I am so glad you have not forgotten me. I was worried that you would not know me anymore and you are my special little sister.'

He picked up the suitcase that Amaiguru Hilda had placed on the ground and, taking my hand as if he was afraid I might run away, he led me onto a small square veranda which had three doors leading off it.

We passed the first room, which was situated on the right arm of the square. It was the kitchen. The first room, at a ninety-degree angle to the kitchen was the sitting room, which we entered. All the doors of the house faced the veranda; there were no interconnecting rooms. I looked around me. The sitting room was a small square room dominated by a red two-piece vinyl sofa and armchair. A small matching coffee table sat in the middle of the room. In one corner was a display cabinet, also red vinyl, with crockery in it and glass doors. On top of the display cabinet was a radio. A sense of relief flooded through me. This must be what Pat's house was like. I sat down on the armchair. Stan disappeared onto the veranda and then emerged again with a glass of Fanta. But I needed to go to the toilet, so Stan placed the drink on the coffee table and led me outside. He pointed to the next room, announcing, 'That is the bedroom,' and then pointed to another door, which was next to the bedroom on the other arm of the square, directly opposite the kitchen. It was a narrow room, no more than four feet wide and six feet deep. At the far end of the narrow room was a round hole with a tin sheet on top. This was the toilet. High up on the ceiling and hanging almost over the hole for the toilet was a large round shower head which dripped cold water with a loud 'ping' as it hit the edge of the tin sheet. I knew that Pat's house was not like this and my heart sank.

As I emerged, I could hear Amaiguru Hilda's voice at the back of the house talking to a neighbour.

'You are so big now,' said Stan, who was waiting for me on the veranda with an expanding smile. 'Do you still understand Shona?' he asked, leading me back into the sitting room and handing me the drink.

I did understand Shona – I probably understood every word that people said on the train and that Amaiguru Hilda spoke to Stan when we arrived – but I was not sure if I could still speak it. I had not uttered a word of Shona in three years. But even if I was still able, I was afraid to speak. It felt

wrong to be speaking an African language. What if someone
told the nuns, who had specifically forbidden us from speaking our mother tongues? I shook my head to protect myself
from the obligation to speak. Stan looked disappointed but
then grinned broadly.

'Never mind,' he said, 'because I can speak English.'

I went on sipping my drink quietly. I did not know what
to say. I was pleased to see Stan, but also confused about
what my relationship with him should be. Not only was he a
male, he was a black male, albeit not yet a man. In all areas
of school life, including the classroom, we were kept well
away from the boys.

That evening Amaiguru Hilda cooked sadza for our
dinner. The mouthwatering aroma of frying meat filled the
little house and my stomach rumbled in response. She served
neat round hillocks of sadza onto three separate plates and
added the meat floating in a rich sauce mixed with green
vegetables. At school I had learnt that sadza was eaten by
'nannies', so I felt uncertain, even though I knew I would
have to eat it, if only because I was ravenous. Stan and I
shared the small two-piece sofa with our plates on the coffee
table, and Amaiguru Hilda sat in the armchair, holding her
plate in her lap. I looked around for a knife and fork.

'Wash your hands in there, Maudie,' Amaiguru said, indicating the dish of water on the floor next to the coffee table.
'Now eat, eat.'

Eating with one's fingers was frowned upon by the nuns –
I could hear Sister Brigitta : 'We do not handle our food with
our hands. That's for savages,' but I saw Stan and Amaiguru
Hilda tucking in, so I washed my hands and joined them.
The food was delicious, better than anything I had eaten at
school. Immediately, I began to feel more relaxed.

Later, Stan and I were sitting outside the house in the
fading evening light and the children who lived in our street

came out, like mice from their holes, to play under the single streetlight. I felt surprisingly happy as we sat on a large rock in Amaiguru Hilda's yard, watching the other children, chatting and laughing. What a relief that Stan spoke English!

'Do you remember when we use to go into the mealie fields and follow the little roads of the field mice?' Stan asked. Three years of re-acculturation had wiped my memory clean of many things. But I pretended that I did remember for Stan's sake. Somehow I felt close to him and reassured by his warm, open manner.

'I use to teach you how to follow the roads, but you were too small to catch the mice yourself. So I use to catch them and we use to take them to the old lady who live in the village. Do you remember her? She was very short because her back was very round and her head was down, down. She was always walking with a stick and she look at us sideways. You remember? You were always feeling sorry for her and every day you say, "Stennie, let's go and catch some mice for Ambuya Zwakaora." Sometimes we use to roast the mice ourself and eat them. You use to say that they taste better than chicken.'

Stan laughed loudly, slapping his hand onto his thigh and throwing his head back with the sheer pleasure of these reminiscences. I was mildly appalled that I should have taken part in such a ritual, something I could never tell my friends at school. I could see Pat's reaction: 'Ach sis, man, how can you eat such kaka?' I imagined the story doing the rounds at school and a shiver of apprehension went through me. But I smiled and said nothing.

'In fact, I use to teach you how to trap birds. They were much more harder than mice, but we use to have so much fun,' Stan continued.

'Are you living with Aunt Hilda now?' I asked the question that had been on my mind since I arrived.

'No, I just came for the school holidays because Amai, she has no money, you see. So Amaiguru said that I should come and help her sell mangoes to the white people and she will give me money to finish my primary school.'

'Are you going to sell mangoes tomorrow?'

'Yes, and you can come with me, because Amaiguru, she will be at work. She said that I must look after you.'

'When am I going to see Mummy?'

'I think Amaiguru is going to take you home very soon. Maybe on Saturday, and I can come with you.'

Seven

Stan was shaking me. I was momentarily disoriented. I was in a single bed in a room I didn't recognise. The walls were bare, with the exception of one small calendar with a picture of a large house, which I realised later was the Matombo Hotel. As soon as Stan's face came into focus, memory flooded back. Amaiguru Hilda was not in the other bed. Seeing my confusion, Stan explained that Amaiguru had had to go to work early.

'I let you sleep today because you are tired. But we have to get up early every day to take the mangoes to the suburbs. Now you must come and have some tea and bread and we can go.'

We walked into town along the same road that Amaiguru Hilda and I had taken the day before. There were children on the street but none of them chased after us shouting 'murungu dhunu'. Perhaps they were afraid of Stan. It was already hot, the blue sky stretching from one end of the world to the other, fading to a light grey where it met the horizon and with only the occasional cloud in between, but Stan took the walk in his stride despite the basket of mangoes, which he carried on his head. He walked quickly, his right arm holding steady the large basket. His blue shirt was tucked neatly into his khaki shorts. He was barefoot. It was a perfect December morning. The air smelt fresh from last night's light rain, which still settled in the potholes, while the cool breeze, dodging and diving between the rows of small houses, made me want to skip. I took little running steps to keep up with Stan and then I stopped to practise my perfect somersaults, prompting him to look at me, annoyance seeping out of every pore. I heard the catch in his voice.

'Are you serious, Maudie? If we don't hurry we will not be able to sell all the mangoes in good time and then we will not be able to go into town.'

That was enough to get me marching, mind focused like a predator. There was a good reason for me to go into town and it had nothing to do with mangoes.

We crossed the railway line and I looked up again at the billboard on the station platform. I wanted to discuss it with Stan, but with so little time to stop and examine billboards, I said nothing. It could wait till later.

I hated the thought of hawking mangoes – or anything else in the white suburbs – but Stan's words the previous evening had opened up a whole new vision of life.

'You know, Maudie,' he had said as we sat on the large rock in front of Amaiguru Hilda's house, 'we should not be so poor when you have a rich father. Maybe he has many farms or businesses. I am sure he can help us.'

I stared at him. Had I heard correctly? I was seven years old and no one had ever talked to me about my actual father. I felt my heart thumping inside my chest like a trapped animal. My voice came out in a whisper, 'Do you know my father?'

'No, but he is a white man. He should help you. He should help our mother, then we would not have to sell mangoes.'

Excitement gave way to hopelessness, then despair.

'But I don't know where he lives, so how can I find him?'

'We just have to look for him. I am sure some of the white people, they will know him.'

It was, for me, a long walk to the suburbs. I was exhausted and ready to give up when Stan announced, 'There is the Matombo Hotel. We must make sure that Amaiguru does not see us, so we will walk on this side.'

The hotel dominated the town. I could not see how Aunt Hilda would be able to see us unless she worked in the hotel itself. Stan had already explained that Aunt Hilda worked as a domestic for a Greek family who owned a bottle store. The family lived above the store, which was not too far from the hotel. We walked quickly and made our way out of town towards the white suburbs.

Stan explained, 'I don't want Amaiguru to see us because we are very late with the mangoes. If we don't sell them quickly, she says that they will get spoilt and people will not buy them and then she will shout at us.'

'Does she like shouting?' I asked.

'Eeh, that one. She is very cheeky,' Stan said shaking his head. Apprehension slid down my throat like hot lava. With my scant knowledge of family life, I felt certain that I would be shouted at daily for making mistakes.

I was flagging when finally Stan walked up to a gate.

'Mango!' he shouted.

I was suddenly embarrassed. I did not want to be seen by white people selling mangoes. It all seemed a little undignified. I stood back from the gate and hid behind the hedge. Dogs barked and I crept further away from the gate. But Stan waited patiently, unafraid, until someone from the house shouted, 'How much?'

'Ten for one shilling, madam.'

He sounded like a professional. I was astounded by his flair and filled with admiration for his guts. We walked from house to house, with me skulking in the background, until all the mangoes were sold. Sometimes it was the owner of the house, often with a little child in tow, who came to the gate, and I stood as far out of sight as possible; sometimes it was the maid or the cook or the gardener, and then I stood with Stan so that I could look over the gate and see the pretty gardens with toddlers on their tricycles speeding along the garden paths or older children jumping and splashing in swimming pools. I was aware that we were visiting areas where only white people lived. Even so, I hoped that none of the children I went to school with would be in one of these houses.

At last, late afternoon, all mangoes sold, we were on our way back to town, walking down the shady avenue lined with jacaranda trees, a few remaining purple fairy-hat-shaped flowers drifting like a sigh and resting resignedly on the ground, creating a macramé carpet. I was tired and needed a rest, so I sat under one of the trees and leaned my back against its trunk, facing the road. I saw a white man emerging from the distance and walking towards us in the centre of the road. I paid no attention. I was not afraid of white people any longer – at school it was black men I was afraid of. But as he got closer, I realised that there was something odd about him. He had the biggest nose I had ever seen. It was crimson with a disconcerting purple tinge and large warts sprouting from it on all sides. It seemed to cover half his face. Stan turned and stared at the man.

'What are you looking at, you little shit? *Voetsak*!' the man spat. Stan turned and, grabbing my hand, he hauled me up, shouting, 'Come, Maudie!' and we ran down the road without looking back, as fast as my legs were able. We ran until we turned the corner and the man was out of sight. We walked to a nearby cluster of gum trees and took cover. No sooner did Stan sit down than he doubled up, shaking. He was writhing on the ground, slapping it with his open hand, shouting *Amaiwe!* with tears running down his face. At first I was panic-stricken, thinking that he had hurt himself. Then I realised he was laughing, and was horrified that he should find it so funny when we had had such a close encounter with this scary man. Stan's laugh was infectious and I started to giggle.

'Do you know that man's name?' asked Stan, struggling for breath.

'No,' I said trying hard not to laugh.

'He is called *Chimuno*,' and soon we were both convulsed with laughter. The idea of someone being called The Nose was a source of great hilarity to us. Stan explained that he was well known and all the black people, including adults, called him by this name.

'Is he dangerous?' I wanted to know.

'Oh no, he is not dangerous.'

I did not feel altogether comforted.

'Then why did he swear and tell you to voetsak?'

'Only because he doesn't like people to stare at him.'

'Then why did we run away?'

'You never know, Maudie. He might have spies who will follow us home and beat us up, or maybe beat Amaiguru.'

I saw the sly smile and found it hard to hide my own.

On our way to town, Stan double-checked to make sure that he had not lost any money. Satisfied, we walked through the town looking at the displays and stopping at the bus station to watch people boarding buses headed for the country.

'Are we going in one of those buses when we go and see Mummy?' I asked, a part of me hoping that the answer would be 'no'. They seemed so crowded, and the tops of the buses were crammed full of a bewildering collection of things, from small boxes to bicycles and even a bed complete with mattress. But Stan said, 'Yes, of course. There is no other way to get home.'

'One day I shall have my own bus,' he added, facial muscles earnest and eyes determined. 'But I have to pass Form Two first and then maybe I can find the money to finish secondary school.'

'Maybe my father can pay for you.'

Optimism seeped into me like honey dripping from a spoon. Today was the day we would start looking for my father. I was sure that we would find him easily and in one day, and all our troubles would be over. Surely there can't be many men named Mr Lenning. Hope filled my head and my chest and sent my spirit soaring. I had no doubt that my father would want to help Stan, who would own a bus when he grew up; maybe even two or three. He seemed so clever and enterprising.

With the limitations placed on African children's schooling, Stan would never complete secondary school. Like the majority of African children, the only government schools he could attend went no further than Form 2. Unless someone came up with the money for him to attend one of the mission schools, he was doomed to low-skilled, low-paid work. While secondary schooling was compulsory for white children and the government provided all the facilities and resources to cater for this, it was voluntary for black children. Secondary schooling up to Form 2 had only been made available to Africans as late as 1940. Most government schools were in urban areas, which had been designated European or white under the Land Apportionment Act. The majority of Africans lived in rural areas set aside for black settlement and if they wanted a school, they had to build it and fund it themselves. According to Reginald Austin (1975), by the end of 1967 only 48 per cent of Africans compared with 88.8 per cent of Europeans had had over ten years of schooling. The number of schools was far short of the demand, as was the quality of education provided. In a racially stratified society where all the laws, whether de jure or de facto, had only one purpose – the maintenance of white domination – black Africans had a glass ceiling that was set very low, with almost no opportunity to break through. The idea was to keep Africans undereducated so that they could service the economy for the benefit of whites.

'Are you going to sell mangoes every holiday?' I asked.

'Maybe, because for secondary I have to go to a boarding school, and it is too much money for Amai.'

I felt a mixture of sadness and hope for Stan and for Amai. I thought about the picture we had painted the previous day of a home with lights and running water, a bathroom and proper toilet. At Amaiguru Hilda's house, a concrete sink stood just outside the kitchen and had to serve for a cornucopia of uses. This was where we got the water for drinking and cooking. This was also where we washed the dishes and the clothes, and where I had to wash my face and brush my teeth in the morning. A hot bath involved filling a large pot with water from the sink and placing it on the primus stove in the tiny kitchen to heat, then transferring it into a small tin bath inside the toilet. The promising-looking shower only produced cold water. Afterwards, any bath water left was used to wash down the floor to minimise smells and keep out flies and this emptied into the hole in the toilet. There were candles and paraffin lamps for lights in the house. All this made it different from what I imagined Pat's house to be like. But even these facilities were luxuries for Amai, though she would probably not have thought about it that way, having always lived a traditional rural life. In our fantasy my father would give Amai enough to build a decent home with running water and lights, and money to pay Stan's school fees and buy uniforms and books – no more hawking mangoes in the white suburbs.

We walked silently for a while. Suddenly the bridge of Stan's nose creased, his small eyes narrowed and, like a panicked rabbit, he grabbed my hand and started to run, saying, 'We must run, Maudie. We will go to the Matombo Hotel. It is lunchtime and the white people will be going there to eat.'

There was a tall tree about twenty metres from the entrance to the hotel.

'I will stand here,' my brother said, moving to the side of the tree furthest from the hotel entrance, 'and you stand there,' pushing me to the side where everyone could see me. 'When you see a white man, go to him and ask him politely if he knows Mr Lenning.'

The doorman, an African in smart hotel livery, black with red velvet edging, was looking at us. I was just about to tell Stan that I could not do it when he hissed, 'Go NOW! Look, there is a man coming – GO,' his finger jabbing me from behind the tree to make me move. I was too slow and with three long strides the man disappeared into the hotel. Another white man stopped to talk to the doorman.

'Go and ask *him*,' my brother said. His fingers were on my back, gently pushing. I took two steps and then turned around and bolted to the safety of the tree.

'Aag,' Stan said, swiping his hand in the air like I was an irritating fly. 'Let's just go home and sort out mangoes.'

I walked forward a few steps then back again to the tree. My head said, just do it! But another persistent voice said, *What if the doorman calls the police? He is suspicious, I can tell. What if a white man pushes me away and I fall or what if someone even claps me? Do I really want to know my father?*

'OK, I'll go to the next man that comes,' I said quickly, before the voice persuaded me to flee. The doorman continued to look at me, yet I felt invisible to the white people. I was about to give up again when I saw a tall man approaching. He stopped and looked at the ground, forehead creased, deep in thought. Then he walked slowly towards the hotel entrance. I found myself striding towards him.

'Excuse me, sir.'

The man folded himself in half, brought his head level with mine and crouched beside me.

'And what can I do for you?'

My heart finally felt settled, my hands no longer needed to cling to the hem of my dress and when he put his arm around my skinny shoulders my throat felt like it was on fire.

'Excuse me sir, do you know Mr Lenning?' I croaked.

'Mr Lenning? Now let me see. Does he live in this town?'

'I don't know.'

'Who is he and why are you looking for him?'

'He's my daddy.'

'Your daddy. I see. I'm afraid I don't know him and if you don't know where he lives, then it's going to be very difficult to find him. Is your mother at home?'

'Yes.'

'Did she ask you to come here?'

'No.'

'Why don't you go home? Talk to your mother, she might know where to find him.'

He smiled as he stood up and, taking my hand, he pressed into it something hard and gently folded my fingers over it. When he patted my head, I felt my throat constrict and tears prickled my eyes. I quickly turned away.

Stan's welcome arm rested magically around my shoulder and I shuffled towards the tree.

'What did he say?'

'He says he doesn't know him. He says we should go home.'

'Don't you want to wait and ask someone else?'

'No, I want to go home.'

I did not try to balance the basket on my head as I had planned to when it finally emptied of mangoes. I barely noticed the sunshine and the open blue sky. Stan's voice blended into all the other sounds around me. The disappointment was profound. Only gradually did I notice the burning feeling in my hand, which was balled up so tightly that releasing my fingers was like taking in a deep breath of air. In my hand was a sixpence. I looked at my brother, who was also gaping at the coin. I took his hand, and placing the sixpence into his palm, I folded his fingers over it.

Eight

The old red Rutendo bus sped along the tarmacked road as we drove through rich farmland. I sat with Stan and Amaiguru Hilda sat behind us. There were miles of green fields with sprinklers dotted here and there. Sometimes we spotted a large house set well back from the fields and the road and partly hidden by tall jacaranda, flamboyant or eucalyptus trees. We were not yet in the Tribal Trust Lands – the land designated by the Land Apportionment Act for African habitation. All the land in the Highlands and the green belt was set aside for white farmers, while most of the land set aside for black people was dry scrub, sandy or rocky – unproductive land. The end of the tarmac was the demarcation line.

We were passing an area of well-drained loamy soil, suitable for tobacco. I was intrigued by the kind of life that was lived within those imposing homes that seemed to be spying on us from behind the trees. I envied the children who were lucky enough to live there and knew that it was a life that I could only dream about.

Soon the tarmac ended and transitioned into a gravel road. Clusters of little thatched houses began to appear. The bus rattled and churned up a thick dust as we bounced and shook like bits of furniture in an earthquake. At first we tried to talk, but our voices vibrated and the noise from the bus forced us to shout at each other, so we kept quiet and Stan resorted to pointing mutely to places or things of interest along the way. The rains had been just right that year, the fields were full of healthy-looking maize standing tall and green against the blue sky. Families were tending their crops, bent double with hoes in their hands. They stopped briefly to stare at the bus going past.

Before long I fell asleep, the semiconscious sleep of someone with chronic insomnia, my head lolling forwards and jerking back so that I sat straight upright like a meerkat. Stan moved closer to the window and, pulling me towards him, he placed my head on his shoulder and his arm around my back to support me. I slept the sleep of a zombie, my mind bouncing from consciousness to unconsciousness in a disturbing miasma of dreams. Then I was wide awake again and Stan was pointing out a small shop on the side of the road.

'That is where we do our shopping,' he shouted into my ear. All I saw was a small square house painted white with a tin roof but with proper glass for windows. On one side of the door was a picture of black children smiling broadly with shining eyes, as if they had won the lottery, and holding up bottles of Fanta; on the other side of the door was a large sign saying *LONDON BAKERY*. The store belonged to the white family that owned the tobacco farm in the area.

'I will bring you there,' Stan shouted again and then turned to look out the window. I nodded. A few minutes later there was a violent shudder and the bus came to a sudden stop. Amaiguru Hilda, Stan and I were the only ones alighting, but there were quite a few people waiting either to get on or to receive parcels sent by relatives who lived in Marandellas.

I stood on the verge and watched Amaiguru Hilda and Stan offload our luggage, not really sure where we were. I was about to call out to Stan and ask, but my thought was interrupted by the sound of ululating. There was a woman doing a little dance in the middle of the yard nearest to where the bus was, her bare feet stamping and kicking up dust. She stopped and, throwing her head up like a cockerel welcoming the dawn, she cupped her hand over her mouth, flapping her fingers and emitting a warm staccato sound like a flock of geese passing overhead. She did another little dance and then started running towards the bus laboriously, like a much older woman, elbows bent upwards and fists moving up and down as if she was sparring with herself. She was slim and wore a dark green, faded dress, which came down to her shins and hung loosely around her waist. Her red doek was tied at the back of her head but was pulled playfully over her forehead. I was startled when she lifted me up and twirled me round, kissing my face and repeating, '*Yowe, mwana wangu.*' She had called me her child – so this was my mother? The sweet smell of woodsmoke wafted from her clothes. There was something familiar and comforting about her smell, her voice, the way she hugged me and kissed my face. I felt happy and smiled as I watched her embracing Amaiguru Hilda and then Stan. She picked up my suitcase with one hand and, taking my hand with the other, she led the way to a round whitewashed house nearby, saying, 'Come, Maudie.'

The room was sparsely furnished with a bed and a small wardrobe. There was barely room for anything else. Time seemed to melt away. I knew this place. Was it the same room? The table and chairs had disappeared, yet it seemed so small. My mother put the case down and Amaiguru and Stan followed with the rest of the luggage.

'Take that box to the kitchen,' Amaiguru Hilda said to

Stan, and he disappeared through the door. I wanted to follow him but felt unsure.

Amaiguru and Amai stood in the bedroom talking. I looked around, wishing the house had been square like the shop we passed. But then I looked at Amai, barely recognising her but feeling her familiarity, and I put my hand in hers. She lifted me up and cuddled me.

'Can you still speak chiZezuru?' she whispered loudly into my ear.

'Aaaah,' Amaiguru Hilda intoned, accentuating and raising the pitch of the final 'ah' as if to emphasise that it was an idiotic suggestion to make of someone so useless. 'Where is she going to speak chiZezuru after three years of not speaking it? She was only four when she went to school.'

'But why don't they help them to keep their language? How are they expected to talk to their families?' Amai asked, flabbergasted.

'They are not allowed to speak Shona, so you might as well forget it and learn to speak English.' Amaiguru Hilda sounded sardonic but they both laughed as we left the bedroom and headed for the other round house, the kitchen, where a girl who turned out to be my sister Abigail was tearing feathers off a lifeless chicken lying in hot steaming water in preparation for our dinner.

I was having a great time in the village. I had reconnected with my cousin and playmate Poona. At first I was shy and not sure if I wanted to go out and play with her, but she took my hand and led me to the guava tree, which we climbed and picked guavas, large and juicy, and then we sat under the tree and ate and Poona talked non-stop in Shona and made me laugh. We took walks to the edge of the vlei and picked long juicy grasses that made gentle farting sounds as we pulled them out of their sheaths. We went about pulling grasses and laughing and looking at each other as if to say, 'Wasn't that a funny one?' until we had had enough and we went back to the guava tree. Poona reacquainted me with the art of plaiting grass and making mats and little baskets. Most of the time I did not say anything, even though I was tempted, but every now and again I answered her questions in single words in Shona. I realised I could speak more than I attempted, but I was still struggling with the fear of speaking a forbidden language, and now that I had said I could not speak it, I was embarrassed to try. Gradually I began to say more, but never in the presence of adults. I did not trust them, not even Amai. I was certain that adults would tell the nuns. Luckily, Amai had a passable understanding of English, although I had never heard her speak it, and I understood Shona.

One day I went to the river with Stan and some of his friends, Poona and her older sister Tamare, an older girl of twelve or thirteen, and a couple of other girls who I had seen but never played with. On the way to the river we picked tsambatsi, which were abundant during the rainy season. Then we collected clay from the riverbed and sat and sculpted, laughing at each other's efforts.

'That one is a funny cow, Maudie. It have very big ears like an elephant, a very long tail like a lion, and short legs like a pig,' teased one girl, and everyone laughed, slapping the palms of each other's hands with a loud smack. When we were tired of the clay, we paddled in the shallows of the river, chasing and splashing each other. I was having the time of my life.

'The girls are going to go for a swim,' Tamare said, to no one in particular. 'Come with us, Maudie.' She said this in English in a tone that indicated that there was no question of my staying with the boys.

'OK,' I shouted, and followed her. We walked some distance from where the boys were until we arrived at a bend in the river. The river dipped, forming a pool which was deep but clear. A clump of trees grew close to the pool and we stripped off our clothes, threw them onto the grass under the trees, and jumped in. The water was soothingly cool. Tamare held my hand and I bobbed up and down and splashed and then she tried to show me how to paddle like a dog. After a while, she called to one of the girls, saying, 'Hold Maudie's hand. I want to have a swim,' and did a dolphin-like dive in the water. I asked the girl to let go of my hand and I continued to splash happily, kicking my legs like Tamare had taught me. Suddenly it seemed as if the noise had disappeared. My face was underwater but my eyes were open and I could see the sun trying to reach me through the water. Then terror seized me, darkness descended and soon I saw nothing more.

'Maudie, Maudie, wake up!' Someone was gripping my shoulder and shaking me. I thought I was dreaming and opened my eyes with difficulty. I was lying on my stomach with my cheek on the grass under a tree. I could feel that I was dressed and my clothes were wet. Gradually I began to make out Stan's face close to mine and then a babble of talk, which got louder each minute. I tried to talk but I coughed instead and only succeeded in making a croaking sound like a sick frog. Stan took me by the waist and helped me sit up. I felt dizzy and weak. There was a group of people around me.

'How are you feeling, Maudie?' Stan asked.

'OK,' I croaked wondering why I felt so strange. I looked around and saw the anxious faces of Tamare, Poona and the others. Memory gradually filtered through the sun's rays twinkling between the leaves.

'No one, no one must say anything about this to anyone,' Stan said, emphasising the 'no one' like a headteacher laying down rules. He looked around.

'Do we all agree?' Everyone was nodding. Gotora, whom every child in the village feared for his violence and bad temper, added gravitas by saying, 'If anyone says anything to anybody, I will make sure they never get to eat sadza again.'

Stan looked at me. 'Maudie,' he said, and his eyes were pleading. 'You must not tell Amai that you were swimming in the deep part today, otherwise she will never let you come and play with us by the river again. You understand?'

I nodded. We sat in the sun for a while to allow my clothes and hair to dry.

'I just turned away for a very short time . . .' one of the girls was saying, when Stan interrupted her with a firm, 'You told us already. Now, we are not going to talk about it again. She's fine, that's all that matters.'

Poona began to pick bits of grass and leaves out of my hair, which must have got there when I was laid out under the tree. Then, urging me to climb onto her back, Tamare led the way home. All I could remember as I clung onto Tamare was the enormous fun I had had. But there was silence in the little group as we walked like a funeral march. Somewhere deep in my psyche the day's events left a mark so menacing that for the rest of my life I have been unable to swim in the sea or in rivers, afraid that a dark and sinister force will pull me away and there will be nothing I can do about it.

Stan woke up just after dawn every morning to milk the cows. One morning I asked him to take me with him. As soon as I heard him calling me, I jumped out of bed, dressed rapidly, and headed out with him to the cattle *kraal*. The air was cool but the sun was already throwing pink streaks across the blue-grey sky.

'Don't put your shoes on, Maudie, because they will be spoilt by the cow dung,' Stan said.

We walked barefoot into the enclosure and I stepped gingerly onto the grass that was interspersed with dry cow dung, avoiding the sour-sweet-smelling fresh dung that lay scattered around the kraal. Other people were moving about among their cows in the adjoining enclosures, talking to them, reassuring them or barking orders.

Stan isolated the cow to be milked from the others. Then he took a rope from his shoulder and expertly threw one end, which had a loop in it, like a lasso around the cow's back legs. Quickly he grabbed the loop and deftly threaded the other end into it. He then pulled the long end, tying the legs together to prevent the cow from moving and kicking the milk can over. He tied the long end to one of the wooden slats that made up the wall of the pen and motioned me to stand near him.

'Do you want to try?' he asked. I hesitated, not sure of myself.

'Come.' He sat me down on a small stool and then positioned himself behind me. With his hands over mine, he placed each hand on an udder just above the teat and pressed down on my hands, squeezing the udder and sliding our hands firmly and alternately over each teat. The milk squirted out, hitting the side of the can with a buzzing sound. We did this several times and then he removed one of my hands and told me to continue with one teat while he milked the other. To my surprise I was milking the cow. I could not wait to tell Amai. It now became part of my daily routine with Stan. Every morning we went to the kraal to milk a cow, accompanied by the welcoming sound of the cockerel and the chattering birds. The odours of the veldt and the cow manure became a part of that pleasurable experience of milking. Sometimes I milked the cow alone while Stan watched and gave directions. Then we went back to the house and had some of the milk, still warm and fresh, in our tea, and hunks of bread, sometimes with a thin spread of jam, before going to the fields.

I had only two weeks of holiday with my mother. I tagged along behind her like a sheep and sat close to her when she was cooking meals, and at night I held on to her as if I was afraid that someone might take her away while I was asleep and when I most needed her. Amai was acutely aware that our time together was limited. She took me wherever she went, but only if I wanted to go. We went to the forest in search of medicinal plants and she explained them patiently – this one for stomachache; this bark is boiled and you drink the water to cure diarrhoea; this one to relieve stress, and so on. Other times we went to the fields where she dug up *tsenza*, a root vegetable like a white carrot, which I loved despite the bland flavour and the fact that, when eaten raw, they turned the teeth brown.

The fields were full of maize at this time of year. I ran through the lines of tall stalks while Amai, Abigail and Stan tended the peanuts, the sweet potatoes, the pumpkins and the other vegetables. As dusk fell, Stan left before us to go and collect the cattle and shut them away in their pen, and Abigail went back to the house to begin preparing the evening meal. Amai and I stayed behind a little longer. She filled a basket with vegetables, showed me how to select the mealies that were ready to be picked, and then we were ready to go home. I walked in front of her, looking at the rows of maize on both sides. This had earlier been my playground but at dusk, with the light fading, the maize looked alien and threatening, as if the long dangling leaves had turned into arms trying to reach out and snatch me. As such thoughts infiltrated my imagination, I slowed down to be nearer Amai. But the path was narrow and Amai was anxious to get home before the darkness enveloped us, so she

73

urged me to walk on in front of her and sang to keep me from my wild imaginings.

Throughout my stay, I was much too busy and too happy to think about my father. But one evening two white men appeared. I recall nothing at all about them except that they sat on the bench in the kitchen and they were laughing. I wondered if one of them could be my father. I did not ask my mother the important question. Perhaps it was late and I was tired. The light in the kitchen was gloomy, as usual, and I have no memory of what they looked like or even of wondering if I looked like one of them. What I do remember was that I felt afraid, perhaps that they were going to take me away, but I never discussed the event with anyone. Only years later did I realise that neither of them could have been my father because my mother told me that she had only ever seen my father once after she became pregnant. They met unexpectedly at the entrance to the magistrate's court. She was entering the court and he was exiting.

'I think he got a shock when he saw me', she said. 'But he only stared briefly while I stepped out of the way, and then he walked out.'

Soon it was time to go back to school. Amai accompanied me to Salisbury and we spent one night with my sister Margie in the servants' quarters at the bottom of the garden behind her employer's house. Abigail and Stan had stayed in the village to look after the home and were themselves overseen by my great-uncle, Sekuru Marondera, and his family – and, no doubt, the rest of the village.

Sisi Margie was slim and quite pretty, like Amai, with small breasts and long, thin legs. The gardener shared her house during the day but at night went off to the township where he lived. Sisi Margie was only sixteen and she was pregnant. Her husband lived in another part of Salisbury.

Sisi Margie's living quarters were small and cramped.

There was a tiny kitchen with no door and Sisi Margie had nailed a large *chitenge*, a traditional cloth from Malawi, over the opening. The kitchen could scarcely hold a table with a primus stove on it. There was a shelf fastened to the wall which held a few items: tin cups and plates and some cutlery. There was barely enough space for two people to sit with outstretched legs on the floor. The bedroom was equally small, with just enough room for a single bed. There was a string with one end tied to the small window and the other end was tied to a nail in the wall. Sisi Margie's maid's uniforms and a few other items of clothes were on hangers, which were hooked over the string. To go to the toilet, one had to go outside and around the back of the bedroom to a little room which had a hole in the ground. To wash herself she had to boil water in the kitchen and transfer it to a small dish which she stood on the floor in the toilet. There she could splash herself and let the water run into the hole in the floor. Tall bamboo plants hid her meagre home from that of her employer. That night, with the employer's permission, Amai and I slept on the floor in the kitchen.

The following morning Sisi Margie asked for the morning off and went with us to the Indian shop in Railway Avenue in town, where she bought knickers, vests and socks to add to my school wardrobe. I wore my 'new' blue smock dress, a hand-me-down from Sisi Margie's employer's daughter. In the evening they took me to the train station, where the nuns were waiting.

Nine

More than a year passed and I did not go home at all. I was in Sister Apollonis' class in Standard 3. I was almost nine years old. Sister Apollonis was telling us a story. I thought that she was an outstanding teacher and no one told a story as well as she did. No one that I knew at school did anything as well as Sister Apollonis. She played several musical instruments, like the organ, the piano, the guitar, the tambourine, the violin and the accordion. She sang too, and formed a church choir, of which I was a member. She was a good painter. Almost forty years after I left the school, I went back to visit and the mural of the world which she had painted in our classroom was still on the wall. She taught us how to paint on ostrich eggs, which she ordered regularly with money sent to the nuns by her family in Austria. Her family also paid for the organ in the new, large, modern-looking church. We were excited and curious when she brought silkworms to the classroom, and we all trundled down to the mulberry trees to pick leaves for their box. This was our science project, in which we learnt all about the life cycle of the silkworm and had the opportunity to observe them spinning their silky cocoons. Sister Apollonis created beautiful designs, and embroidered the altar cloths for the church. She taught us to sew and decorate small items like handkerchiefs and to knit, playing classical music while we worked. I had never heard such music before. One of my favourite pieces of music was 'The Blue Danube'. But not satisfied only with things Austrian or German, she taught us Scottish country dancing. I lived for Tuesday afternoons when we met on the concrete quadrangle that was bordered by the classrooms and I was transported by a form of dance a world away from my experience. One day Sister told us that we had such aptitude for Scottish dancing that she had brought a surprise. She opened a large box in the classroom and it was full of costumes that she explained were traditional for Scottish dancing. I remember long skirts or dresses and little waistcoats. She handed each one of us something to wear, and we were no longer African children learning to dance a foreign dance, but made to feel like Scottish children hopping, skipping and twirling to the sounds of our Gaelic culture. She told us about the Surprise Packet Company, a company that she said was responsible for the gifts we found in our desks when we had worked hard or achieved well or made improvements in behaviour. The only thing that Sister Apollonis did not get involved with was sport. With her as my form teacher, I looked forward to lessons with such excitement that I could hardly wait to get to class. I hated it when our lessons were interrupted – I did not have to worry about disruption – no child would have wanted, let alone dared to disrupt Sister Apollonis' lessons.

I was riveted by the story she was telling about the time she and two other nuns escaped from the Mau Mau in Kenya. But today there was an interruption. Sister Frances poked her head through the door and Sister Apollonis went to see her. Then they both turned and looked at me, and Sister Frances gestured to me to follow her. My heart lurched. Why was I being called? Had I done something wrong? But I was also annoyed about missing the rest of the story and dragged my feet, my face distorted with a frown.

'Sister, please can I come later? I don't want to miss the story.'

'No, you must come right away. Go to the dormitory, there is someone waiting for you.'

I walked right past the black woman sitting on the floor at the entrance to the girls' dormitory. I never received visitors. I had no idea who might have come to see me. The woman was calling my name softly, 'Maudie, Maudie.' I turned. The woman was stretching her arms out to me. It was my mother. I fell into her arms and she held me and kissed me all over my face. I was not sure if this was allowed, and I was afraid that the nuns might see her holding me and I would get into trouble. But I did not resist. I was so happy to see Amai that all fear of what the other children might say disappeared. She seemed to me to be exactly the same as the last time I had seen her, except that she wore smart clothes like Amaiguru Hilda, a knee-length light blue skirt with flowers on it, a white blouse, and a bright scarf tied neatly around her head. She also wore shoes, comfortable flat shoes. I had not seen her wear any shoes during my last visit to the village. I stayed with her for the rest of the day. Parents were usually allowed to visit at weekends, but as the school was some way off the beaten track, the rules were flexible if parents came from far away and relied on public transport. My mother wanted to see me and took the first opportunity she had to make the long journey. I walked around the school with her, leaving only to go and have my lunch and dinner. The other children stared but no one said anything. By now it had become clear to me that nearly all the children in the school had at least one parent or a grandparent or other antecedent who was an indigenous black African.

I now understood what it meant to be a Coloured in Rhodesia.

Amai had her meals in the maids' quarters. The parlour was only for 'special' visitors – we all knew and took for granted that this meant European, light-skinned or well-off Coloured visitors. Communication was stilted because, although I understood Shona, I would not speak it. Partly that was because I was afraid I would be told off, but also partly because I was in denial. I noticed that those who spoke Sindebele were neither ashamed nor afraid to speak their language privately, whereas it was rare for me to hear any of the children speaking Shona. As I understood Shona, and Amai understood some English, we were able to communicate, and I was happy. After lunch I was allowed to miss afternoon activities and so I joined her in the maids' quarters. We were sitting at a table in a small room. There was no one else present. I paid little attention to my surroundings as I was distracted by the sweets Amai had brought. I was also curious to know what had been happening at home.

'Why didn't Stan come with you?' I asked, my mouth full and dribbling sweet saliva, which I sucked up noisily.

'He must look after the home and also we don't have any money for him to come.'

'Is he still at school?'

'No, there is no money to send him to school.'

'But Stan said he wanted to go to secondary school and then he could work and buy a bus,' I said, indignantly, as if Amai was the obstacle to his ambitions.

'There is nothing we can do when there is no money. But if Margie and Abigail can help, then he will finish secondary school.'

'But why doesn't my daddy give you some money to pay for him?' Amai looked at me, surprised. I had never mentioned my father to her and she had not discussed him with me. She stared at me for some time. I began to fidget uncomfortably,

80

certain that I had said something wrong. Then she took my hand and, stroking it as if the idea of a father was a stain she needed to clean off, she said, 'Your father died when you were about three years old.'

It was my turn to gape at my mother. I was shaken by this news. I had invented stories about how my father was building a beautiful new house for my mother on a farm and that when I finally left Bushtick, he was going to take me and my mother and brother to live with him and help my brother to buy a bus. Now I would have to say that he had died and that there was no future for me or my brother. Amai saw the distress on my face.

'He was a very good man,' she said gently. 'He took us, you and me, everywhere with him; even to the Victoria Falls. I would never have seen the Victoria Falls and the Zimbabwe Ruins if it hadn't been for him. And he didn't care about "this is for white people; this is for black people" – I always sat in the front seat with you when we travelled.'

I did not understand what she meant when she talked about sitting in the front or the back, and I did not care. I was disappointed and angry. How could he die when there was so much for him to do?

'But are you always going to stay in the village?' I asked tearfully, still clinging to the dream that somehow my mother might manage to move to a Western-style house with electricity and running water.

'Yes, it is my home. That is where I want to stay.'

I gawped, flabbergasted. How could she be happy to live like that? I had thought that Amai would welcome the chance to leave the village and not have to work in the fields. I was confused and did not say anything. I turned away so that she would not see my eyes, which had filled up and were about to overflow.

'Come here, Maudie,' Amai said, pulling me to her chair

and standing me between her knees. She held my hand with one calloused hand and stroked my hair with the other.

She tried to sound cheerful. 'Your father liked you so much. He was the one who gave you the name Maudie, after his sister. He used to buy you very pretty clothes and toys. I never wanted for anything.'

'But why did he stop looking after me?' I asked, not quite ready to forgive him.

'Because your grandmother and I and all the children had to leave my sister's farm, where we were living. He lived in a caravan nearby because he was building roads in the area. There were problems in our family.' It was all too much for me to take in. I could not understand why she had to leave him; why she did not try to stay in touch; why she did not go back to see him; why he did not visit her; why grown-ups make such stupid decisions – and now he was dead. I did not ask any more questions. There did not seem to be much point. Instead I asked, 'Am I going home for the Easter holidays?'

'I don't know,' she replied. 'We will have to see what the Sisters say.'

It was almost bedtime. Sister Brigitta, our new boarding mother since Sister Dagoberta retired, came to fetch me from the maids' quarters, where Amai was having her supper. I had had my supper much earlier with the other children.

'Sister, where will my mummy sleep?'

Sister Brigitta looked at the maids as if it was their decision.

'We will make a bed for her in the laundry because there is not enough room here,' one of the maids said, looking directly at Sister Brigitta.

Something did not seem right to me, but I said nothing. Only the older girls were allowed in the laundry, so I assumed it was a special type of room. I sat close to Amai. It was as if

I was afraid that if I did not feel her physically close to me, she might disappear and I might never see her again.

'Come, child,' Sister Brigitta said, 'it is nearly time for bed, and you must join the other children.'

I started to cry and cling to Amai, and Sister Brigitta said impatiently, 'I can let you stay a few more minutes, but then you will have to come with me.'

I cheered up immediately and snuggled closer to Amai. The maids laughed and Sister Brigitta looked heavenwards, made a 'tssk' sound and walked out into the dusk.

The laundry room was in the square, which housed the kitchen and the nuns' living quarters. We crossed a small vegetable patch along one side of the maids' quarters, stepped down a low kerb and passed the large tree with a bench beneath it where one of the old nuns could be seen sitting at most times of the day and evening, fingering her rosary beads and moving her mouth rapidly as she said her Hail Mary.

The laundry was a rectangular room with large windows and equally large concrete sinks under the windows. Next to the sinks were two peculiar metal 'machines' with rollers, and wheels on the side for turning the rollers. When I was an older pupil and allowed to go into the laundry, I learnt that these were mangles for squeezing the water out of the washing. Against the wall opposite the sinks and mangles were large white bags suspended from hooks and touching the floor. The centre of the room was dominated by a long concrete table with various items on it like cloths, soap, pegs, and other things that held little interest for me. It looked like a space where everything was kept in its place, and smelt clean and fresh. I was fascinated by the laundry room, mainly because it was usually out of bounds. It seemed so full that I wondered where Amai would sleep. Perhaps she would be allowed to sleep in the boarding house with me. Then two maids came in hauling a mattress, which they placed under the table. A jolt like an electric shock went through me, not because Amai had to sleep on the floor but because she was going to sleep under the table in this cold, damp room with big white bags watching her like silent ghosts. I clung to her and she squeezed me and said, 'Let me go now so that I can make the bed.'

When Sister Brigitta came back, I asked her why my mother could not sleep in the dormitory as someone else's mother had been allowed to do some weeks earlier.

'You know we don't have room in the boarding house,' she snapped. 'Now come along. I have already bent enough rules for you today.'

A few weeks earlier, the mother of one of the older girls visited her daughter. Because she had travelled a long distance and could not return home that same day, a bed was placed against her daughter's bed and she spent the night with her daughter in the dormitory. The girl's mother laughed and joked with Sister Brigitta, her caramel skin only a shade darker than the nun's. *Sister Brigitta must not like me*, I thought. She must not like my mother. My mother was a nanny. Perhaps that was the reason why she was making my mother sleep in the laundry room. Could it also have been that she did not like me because she did not get on with Sister Apollonis, and Sister Apollonis was my favourite teacher?

I never found out. I was upset, but followed her meekly, knowing that it was pointless to argue or make a fuss.

I joined Pat, who was playing a hand-clapping game with Shirley. The light had faded, sending furtive but exhilarating messages through the hemisphere.

'Come and play threes,' Pat said, but I declined, unable to summon up a smile for my friend.

'What's the matter?' Pat asked. It was as if she had opened the stopcock to my suppressed emotions. I burst into tears. Pat put her arm around me and said, 'Has your mummy gone already?' I shook my head.

'Then what?' she said with some impatience.

'My daddy died,' I said, sniffing and heaving with sorrow. I tried hard to summon up images of a dead father but found it impossible to dismiss the sight of Amai making her bed under the table in the laundry. I was too ashamed to tell anyone, not even my best friend. A few other girls came and soon I was surrounded.

'Shh,' Pat whispered to them. 'Her daddy died.'

'Shame, shame,' I heard several mouths whisper. That only made me cry harder. It was time to go to bed. Sister Brigitta appeared.

'What's going on here?' she asked.

'Sister, Maud's daddy died,' Pat offered helpfully.

'But she doesn't know who her daddy is. Did your mother tell you this?' she said, taking my hand from my face. I nodded in between sniffs and hiccups. She turned to the other girls.

'All of you go inside now. It's time for bed.'

She held my hand while the other girls dispersed.

'Now stop that crying. Your mother should not tell you such things.'

She held my upper arm and shepherded me into the cloakroom.

'Now sit here,' she said with a hint of kindness. 'You can go to bed when you are feeling better.'

When she came back, I was sitting on the floor with my knees drawn up, my arms around my legs and my head on my knees. She took my hand and then pushed me into the dormitory, fingers digging gently into my back, and I made my way to my bed with the night-light to guide me. The other children were in bed. One or two popped their heads up like little iguanas, smiled at me and then quickly ducked down again when Sister Brigitta came to check on me.

Amai left the next day. Sister Apollonis allowed me to miss the first lesson so that I could go with her to the gate.

85

There was a burning feeling in my chest and throat, and sharp prickles behind my eyes as I watched her walking out – there was no one to give her a lift, so it would be a long walk to the main road where she would have to hitchhike to Essexvale or, if she was lucky, to Bulawayo in order to catch a lift or the bus back to Salisbury. The image of her lonely figure walking away from the school gate lives permanently in my mind. I longed to go with her just to keep her company.

Later that day as I helped Sister Apollonis clear up in the classroom, I said, 'Sister, why did my mummy sleep in the laundry? Sheila's mummy slept in the dormitory when she came.'

Sister Apollonis bristled. She looked at me.

'Who put her in the laundry?'

'Sister Brigitta.'

Sister Apollonis patted my head with a faraway look, then, as if suddenly remembering that I was there, she turned, her face soft and her eyes misty. She said, 'She probably thought it best to give your mother some privacy. I'm sure your mother was all right and didn't mind much.'

On Saturday morning, as I was heading out with the other children for games on the sports field, Sister Brigitta called me. She took me into the cloakroom and pointed to a pile of shoes belonging to the 'babies'. There was a tin of polish, a shoe brush and a cloth, and she said, 'You will not have games today. You will sit here and polish all these shoes. If they are not sparkling, you will have to do them again. That will teach you to question my decisions and to talk to other people about them.'

Ten

The Christmas holidays arrived. Amaiguru Hilda met me at the train station and I spent a week with her before going home to my mother. That visit to Amaiguru Hilda was full of surprises. The first was that she had moved to a different township. Her new house had two bedrooms, a sitting room, a kitchen and a small veranda, and to my surprise and delight, it had electricity. Everything else was the same as the old house, including the absence of hot water. The toilet was still a hole in the ground, and there was an overhanging cold shower, and a small tin bath into which one had to pour hot water, this time heated on a small electric two-plate burner that took just as long as the primus stove but was more expensive to run. But at least one could get light by simply flicking a switch. The sitting room was furnished with the same familiar red-vinyl two-piece suite with its matching coffee table, and the same display cabinet with glass doors where Amaiguru kept her crockery.

Amaiguru Hilda had moved to this house because of the second surprise – she had a husband. The man was Mr Shiri, who worked at the Matombo Hotel; a divorcee who had brought with him his two children. His former wife lived in Malawi, but I did not know or ask for the reasons why the children had left their mother. Amaiguru now had two step-children: Albert, a boy of nine, and Pamela, who was two years younger.

There was a third and even bigger surprise. There was another little girl called Morsia, about six years old, who Amaiguru told me was my sister, my mother's youngest child whom Amaiguru had adopted. She was tiny for her age and skinny, with big melancholy eyes and a sweet, round, dimpled face.

'This one I got from your mother when she was a baby,' Amaiguru said, placing her hand on Morsia's head, as if she was talking about a table. 'Some women know how to have babies but don't know how to look after them.'

I knew that this heavily loaded statement was about my mother, and although it made me feel sad and confused, I didn't understand it enough to feel angry or resentful.

I looked at Morsia, who was staring up at me with an unreadable expression on her face. I had no recollection of having seen Morsia before, and surely I would have seen a four-year-old child two years earlier, when I first came to stay with Amaiguru Hilda, unless she had been visiting our cousin Goodwill, Amaiguru's son. With Amaiguru Hilda's demanding job as a maid, it made sense to send Morsia to spend the holidays with cousin Goodwill – a headteacher who was kind and had a sense of humour that children could understand. But why would my mother not have said anything? Unless she had, but as a seven-year-old who was trying to get used to having a mother again, perhaps I had not taken much interest and had forgotten. I thought about Amaiguru's statement. Could it be true? My mother had, after all, given me away to the nuns. Perhaps she had also given Morsia away. In any case, here Morsia was, looking forlorn and timid.

A seed of resentment against Amaiguru was, however, sown on that day. Over the coming years, and as I got to know Amai better, I began to detach emotionally from Amaiguru Hilda for her frequent and often uncalled-for criticisms of Amai. There were times when she was downright hateful, calling my mother a whore or belittling her for being illiterate. I learnt from my sister Margie that Amaiguru had asked Amai to bear a child for her and that Morsia was the result. Many years later, Morsia herself talked about how Amaiguru would not let her go to the village because she did not want her to find out who her biological mother was. She grew up believing that our mother was her aunt. Amaiguru's comments about Amai upset me and I grew not only to resent but also to distrust her.

It was only on a visit to Zimbabwe in 2006 when Amaiguru Hilda was old and frail that I softened towards her. She lived with her son and daughter-in-law in one of the former European suburbs. She was skinny and looked as if she had shrivelled to a little over half her former height. The top of her head was now level with my shoulders, when barely eight years earlier she had been a little taller than me. She wore a simple dark green dress with a matching headscarf and comfortable black shoes. She sat upright as she had always done, but this time she needed a walking stick to help raise her from her sitting position. But she had not lost any of her pride and self-possession. She still talked with an air of authority, summoning my friend, a giant of a man to her slight frame, with, 'Come here, my boy.' Her eyes had deteriorated. One of them gave her constant pain, so that she was unable to read her Bible for long periods and she sat in the sitting room or in her bedroom day in and day out with nothing to do. She looked half-starved and said that her diet consisted of a bowl of porridge once a day, but she would not go into details about the reasons for such a meagre diet.

When I was a child, it was her treatment of Morsia in particular that angered me. Although I did not like spending time at Amaiguru Hilda's, I was often relieved to have gone because of the difference it seemed to make to Morsia. Her downcast face would visibly alter over the course of the week or so that I would stay. Morsia did not seem to have any friends, especially as Albert and Pamela – older, and no doubt missing their mother – were always together, and Amaiguru largely left them to their own devices. Whenever I came from school I brought toys which, as one of the poorer children at the school, I received from the Lions Club or the Moss family, who lived in Bulawayo and were patrons of Sacred Heart Home. I shared these with Morsia, which provided her some respite from loneliness and drudgery.

On the first evening of my arrival and after we had had our dinner, Amaiguru said, 'Go outside and play now, before it gets dark.'

We were just about to walk out when she said, 'No, not you Morsia, I need you to help me.'

Morsia stayed indoors and washed the dishes and tidied up. By the time she had finished, it was dark and we had to go back indoors. The next day I noticed that this was the pattern of Morsia's life. It was, 'Morsia, go and fetch such and such; Morsia, go and tidy up the bedroom; Morsia, sweep the bedroom floor; Morsia, pick up the rubbish in the yard.' My little sister was a drudge, a modern-day Cinderella, and she was only six years old. On one occasion, I offered to help with the washing-up, but Amaiguru stopped me, declaring, 'She needs to do the housework herself. Who do you think will help her when you are away at school?'

I was too scared to ask why Albert and Pamela were not given tasks when they lived there permanently. Amaiguru Hilda had a caustic tongue. And yet she was not entirely without charm. One evening she decided to do all the clearing up herself, while all of us, including Morsia, went out to play.

'You can come in now,' she called, and we went in, intrigued because it was not quite bedtime yet. The kitchen was pristine.

'Today we are going to have a story before bed,' she said, looking at us with a smile. She was a good storyteller, and transported us to dark forests where the spirits of ancestors and of the animals of the jungle led us to magical places where children in particular were precious, valued beings. We did not see the intrinsic paradox that lay between Amaiguru Hilda's treatment of Morsia and the enchanted lives of the children in her story. Even if we had, we would not have dared to question it. Her mission, I gathered much later, was to teach Morsia *tsika*, the customs and traditions of the Shona people, which would enable her to conduct herself anywhere comfortably. Morsia was an African child and Amiguru Hilda's responsibility. Not only was I a Coloured, but I had already been ruined by going to school, where I was forbidden to speak my mother tongue or follow the traditions of my African ancestors. I was now the responsibility of the nuns. Albert and Pamela had a different Malawian culture and were Mr Shiri's responsibility.

When it was time to go home to the village, I travelled alone for the first time. Amaiguru told the bus driver where to stop for me and, standing in the doorway of the bus, she entreated the passengers with, 'Eh, look after my daughter for me, please, and help her get off when she arrives in Bumburwi.'

She spotted someone she knew and shouted, 'Eh, Mai Rudo, how are you? Look after our daughter for me, won't you?'

Morsia stood with Amaiguru, looking forlorn. My chest felt tight and I choked back the tears. Amaiguru had said 'No' to our pleas for Morsia to go to the village too.

'There is no one to bring her back from the village and we still have to buy her school uniforms and books. I can't take time off from work to do all these things and to come and fetch her from the village.'

Amaiguru was right, of course. I would be going to Salisbury at the end of my stay and Morsia would have to be taken to Marandellas.

Morsia had then pleaded with me, 'Don't go, please. Please don't go.'

But I wanted to go home. I wanted to see my mother, my brother, Sisi Margie's child, Tanda, and my friends before going back to school. There was nothing I could do. Then suddenly, as if I had had a brainwave, I ran down the gangway and, standing in the doorway of the bus, I held out my hand and gave Morsia one of my favourite toys, a baby doll, one of a collection of gifts from the Moss family.

Morsia, who had no toys of her own, beamed, her round face looking like a full moon and with the biggest smile, her dimples like craters. She had played with this doll throughout the week of my stay, and it had brought her so much joy. I had felt bad taking it away. Her face was that of a child again as she hugged the little doll close to her chest, her eyes shining. She still had the smile until the bus moved off and I could no longer see her.

Many years later, in England, Morsia and I chatted about that particular holiday and the doll I had given her.

'You won't believe what happened to that doll,' she said.

'What?' I said, looking at her quizzically.

'I don't know what I did, but as a punishment Aunt Hilda took the doll away and threw it into the fire.'

I stared at her, shocked. She shrugged her shoulders, simultaneously twisting her mouth to one side as if to say, 'What can I say. That's how it was.' I was even more shocked when she recounted other examples of emotional abuse that she had suffered. She had never told anyone about them.

The minute I alighted from the bus at Bumburwi, I felt at home. Poona ran to the bus and hurled herself at me with a force that almost knocked me off my feet.

The sound of the cockerel got Amai out of bed like clockwork at dawn every day. As a woman without a husband, and with only thirteen-year-old Stan to help her, she performed all the tasks of the home, including, on school days when Stan was briefly at Waddilove School, milking the cow, fetching water and letting the chickens out of their coop and feeding them with corn. She also had Tanda, my sister Margie's three-year-old, to take care of. She was soon to take the baby, Sinikiwe, as Sisi Margie was not allowed to have her children with her at her employment. This time I shared a room with Stan and slept on a pile of blankets on the floor in the kitchen. Amai slept with Tanda. I was generally aware that Amai was up and would hear her waking up Stan. I would either fall asleep again or doze until Amai called me to get up. Usually by the time I had woken up, around 7 a.m., Amai had swept the yard (which I sometimes offered to do but did badly) and washed all the dishes, which were left overnight to be washed in the morning on a stand outside the kitchen because they could not be done in the dark. She had collected water, made a fire, boiled water for tea and for washing and washing-up, fixed up something for breakfast – sometimes an egg and, if we were lucky, bread and jam, but usually leftovers from the night before. She had also started preparing the food to take with her to the fields – often a bean stew known as *mutakura*. Filida, Margie and Abigail, having left home to work in town or to get married, Amai's life was now a continuous series of chores. The only job I recall her asking me to do was to help with getting breakfast for Tanda. After breakfast we would be on our way to the fields where, apart from a short break after a meagre lunch, Amai and Stan worked until dusk. I played with and generally took care of Tanda. When it was our household's turn, Stan watched the village cattle in the vlei. Now that I was nine years old and if it was a Sunday, I was allowed to spend my day watching the cattle with Stan. Days like these were the most fun. A few people in the village made the long trek to the church service in Waddilove or at Border Church, where there was a Methodist mission. I do not recall that my mother went to church, but it may be that I was so preoccupied with my friends and wandering in the bush, climbing trees or swimming that I would not have known what she did. She was certainly not as fervent a Christian as Amaiguru Hilda. Perhaps her role as a 'svikiro' or spirit medium when she was said to communicate with a dead uncle was at odds with Christian practice. I was oblivious to all this at that time. Sundays were days of rest, fun, friends and 'incidents'.

It was the Sunday before I went back to school. I was with my friends Poona and Tamare. We had gone to gather hute berries, which hung in abundance like bunches of grapes from the *mukute* trees. I started to run, spindly legs leaping over the tall grass, and I paid no heed to Tamare's shouts for me to wait. The need to compete, to be first to get the fruit and the first to fill my basket, drove me in the same way that I felt driven at school to be top of the class or the first to gather the mulberries when the nuns allowed us to climb the trees. Poona had no interest in competing and strolled along nonchalantly, enjoying the walk, the chatter, the beautiful day. I arrived at the tree and started to climb, ignoring Tamare's warnings to stop. I sat down on a branch and stretched my arm out to a large bunch of fruit, and then I saw it. It was dark green and seemed to have coiled itself along the branch as far as my eyes could see, head disappearing into the leaves. I had almost put my hand on it. My screams could be

94

heard all the way from the river to my mother's house as I lost my balance and fell.

'I told you to stop,' scolded Tamare as she carried me home on her back. Poona had my shoes, which I could no longer wear because my ankle had begun to swell.

I felt wounded when Tamare mocked me by saying, 'You are not a village girl – you are a town girl and you have a lot to learn. Mukute is a favourite place for black mambas. You are lucky that it didn't eat you.'

I was silenced and ruminated over my good fortune. My ankle may have hurt, but at least I had escaped with my life!

Eleven

For the following three years, from 1960 to 1962, I went home for the holidays, except that home did not mean the village – it simply meant away from school. A pattern was established where I travelled to Salisbury on the train with the other children and was met by whoever was taking care of me for the first part of the holiday. After that I would be shunted elsewhere, and then finally sent for a week or so with my mother before I went back to school. The rationale for this, Amaiguru Hilda told my mother, was that as a ward of the government, I was not allowed to spend long periods of time in the village – presumably in order not to undo the nuns' attempts to civilise me.

During those years I spent some of my holidays with cousins, the Bhanas, on their farm outside the asbestos-mining town of Shabani in the south of the country. I was happy there, unlike on a holiday I spent with another set of Coloured relatives in Salisbury. This uncle was my mother's cousin. While my uncle was at work, his wife would take her children visiting or to town, leaving me behind with the maid. The first time that it happened, in 1960, I went wandering around Arcadia, the area designated for Coloured residents, where my uncle and his family lived. I knew no one and was lucky to bump into Moira, a girl who was older than me but who also went to Bushtick. Her mother took me in and fed me and then, later that evening, Moira took me back to my uncle's house. After that I went to Moira's house every day until it was time for me to be moved on to another relative.

My holiday experiences, both good and bad, left me with a feeling of impermanence and of being the outsider always looking in, forever grateful for the smallest acknowledgement or insignificant kindness. The experience at my uncle's house left me wary. I felt that I belonged nowhere and although I was shown many kindnesses, I also felt that people had a right to be unkind to me. Somehow I deserved it. I was unwanted and unlovable. But these experiences also left me with a sense of self-reliance – an understanding that while I was dependent on many different people for many things, it was up to me to make things happen in my life. I was the only one who could decide my own fate. That was something I only discovered at secondary school, when I felt that I could say 'no' to some of the decisions made for me. In the meantime, I was batted from one relative to another, and my time in the one place I would have liked to be, namely with my mother and my brother Stan, was severely restricted. And so, caught between so many different identities – my African family and their traditions and beliefs, Coloured relatives and friends with their mixture of African and Western cultures, the German and Austrian nuns and Catholicism – I struggled with my own. I longed to belong, anywhere – as long as I was a full and acknowledged member of that community. When I reflected on this, I realised that the place I was least likely to feel a sense of belonging was with a white father. By age ten I understood enough of the politics of the country, thanks to Amaiguru Hilda, to know that I could never be a part of the white community – unless it was a community of nuns. But that, as far as I was concerned, did not count, and a nun was something I did not want to be. One day our teacher gave us a list of words out of which we had to choose six and write one sentence for each. In the list was the word 'vagabond'. When I saw the dictionary meaning of the word, I was wracked with pain and self-pity – 'a wanderer, a person with no fixed home, a beggar or thief'. I wrote the sentence, 'I am a vagabond because I have no fixed home, but I am not a beggar or a thief,' just so my teacher, who knew my lifestyle, made no mistake.

I always went 'home' every year during the Christmas holidays. But one year, Christmas 1962, I was not sure what arrangements had been made for me, and Sister Frances had had no information. I stood and watched the children who were travelling by train as they piled into the school bus to be taken to Bulawayo. Several cars arrived and were parked in the space in front of the dining room and the parlour. Families were carrying suitcases and children were shouting their goodbyes to each other. I waved to those who were being taken by school combi to Bulawayo station and was walking back to the girls' boarding house when someone called me and told me that Jenny was looking for me. I started walking back towards the car park. Jenny saw me and came running towards me. She said, 'My mummy wants to see you.'

I was delighted and excited, assuming that this was recognition of my friendship with Jenny.

The car was parked in front of the parlour with all the doors open and Jenny's mother and aunt were packing suitcases and bags into the boot. As we approached, the two women stopped what they were doing.

'Mummy, here's Maud,' Jenny said, before going to sit in

the car. Jenny's mother and aunt leaned against the fender and beckoned me to them.

'What's your surname?' her mother asked.

I was overcome with shyness and with eyes cast down I answered politely and formally.

'My surname is Lenning.'

'Is that with an "a" or an "e"?' she quizzed.

'With an "e".'

'Where is your daddy?'

Somehow I did not feel like telling them that he was dead.

'I don't know,' I said.

'Is he a European?'

'Yes.'

'Do you have any brothers and sisters?'

'Yes.'

'Do they have the same daddy as you?'

'No.'

'Are they Africans?'

'Yes.'

'Where were you born?'

'In Enkeldoorn.' This last piece of information, which I had received from the nuns, turned out to be false.

Jenny's mother and aunt turned from me and said something to each other. I waited. Jenny was still in the car. Her mother looked at me kindly and said, 'OK, thank you.'

I started walking back to the boarding house, disappointed and puzzled. I had been secretly hoping that they might invite me to go on holiday with them. As we had walked to the car, I had begun to fantasise about going on holiday regularly with her family and experiencing the kind of life I so longed for in a house with several bedrooms, electricity, running water and a flushing toilet. If that had not been the intention, then what was all the questioning about?

When Jenny came running after me and accompanied me halfway back to the boarding house, I asked her.

'Why was your mummy asking me all those questions?'

'She wanted to know if you were related to us.'

'Am I?'

'No, my mummy doesn't think so, because her daddy's name is Lanning with an "a" and your name is Lenning, with an "e".'

So I might even have been related to them! What an injustice it was that I was Lenning and not Lanning. One letter made the difference between having a father who would surely take an interest in me and look after me and one who was dead and would never come for me. Jenny and I walked together in silence. We never pursued the subject again.

Twelve

I was in Standard 4A and Pat was in Standard 4B. We did not see each other as often as we used to. Jenny, who was in my class, was my new friend. But Pat and I often formed a pair as we lined up to go to the dining room for our meals. Pat was less talkative; she seemed to have coiled into herself since she came back from the Easter holidays. One evening as we waited to walk down to the dining room, Pat said, 'Can you keep a secret?'

'Uhuh,' I replied vaguely, my mind distracted by a movement in the lemon hedge that turned out to be a cat. Pat always had secrets. 'Maud, this is a very, very big secret. You can't tell nobody.'

Her tone, unusually solemn, made me pay attention.

'I won't,' I said with more interest.

'Say my livin,' she said, making a cross over her heart with her forefinger and then pointing to the sky.

'My livin God,' I said, licking my forefinger, making a cross over my heart and then pointing to the sky as she had done.

'Coz if you tell, I'll get in such trouble with my mummy, isn't it?'

'My livin – I won't tell.' I reassured her by flicking my wrist so that my fingers knocked against each other and produced a snapping sound. Pat leant over and, putting her mouth over my ear, she whispered, 'My daddy is in jail,' and then looked down as if she was about to cry.

'Why?' I asked.

Pat shrugged her shoulders, then turned away to close the subject.

'I swear I won't tell nobody,' I said, and left it at that. But immediately my thoughts went to my father. Could he be in jail? Did Amai say he was dead because she did not want me to know that he was in jail? Maybe if he was in jail I would be able to see him. Was it possible to see someone who was in jail? No, of course he wouldn't be in jail. He was a European, and as far as I knew, European people did not go to jail. The whys and wherefores of that were too difficult and complicated for me to bother about. He was dead and I needed to get used to that. In any case, Pat was so upset about her father that going to jail, I thought, must be the worst thing in the world. Would I have wanted that for my father just so I could know where he was?

After supper, during play hour, Tresa, the school bully, and her cronies went around as usual telling the 'big' girls – those aged ten and above, to gather at the bottom of the playground, furthest from the entrance to the boarding house where the Sister on duty sat reading and paying little attention to anyone, unless they were hurt or someone came to report on something. Pat and I walked slowly to the end of the playground. Tresa was one of the oldest girls in the school and this was her final year of primary school.

'I really hope she doesn't pick me,' I said apprehensively.

'She won't pick you,' Pat reassured me, 'coz just one blow and all your bones will break,' she teased. 'Anyway, if she picks you and me, I'll run away. I'll go all the way home to Bulawayo and tell my mummy.'

I was not reassured.

In the dusky evening when the soft light speaks of settling down, of peace, of rest, Tresa ordered us to form a big, tight ring and to clap and sing loudly. A sweet evening scent wafted from the lemon hedge, but we barely noticed it, minds focused on following Tresa's orders for the sake of self-preservation. She then selected two girls, usually best friends, placed them in the centre of the ring and ordered them to fight while the rest of us sang and clapped our hands to shield the activity from Sister. When the winner was declared, they had to join the others singing and clapping and two more girls were selected. We continued this grotesque performance until bedtime, each girl dreading the possibility that she might be the next to go into the ring.

Tresa walked over to Pat and took her hand. I was filled with dread because if she selected me to fight with Pat, we could never be friends again. Tresa would not tolerate any pretend fighting and I was sure to get a solid beating from the feisty Pat. The bully looked at me and I started shaking, ready to cry. Thankfully, she passed me by and selected another girl, Monica, older and taller than Pat.

At first, the two girls stood in the centre of the circle looking at each other, fists ready, but without antagonism, more like two people who had met once before and were trying to remember each other's names. Tresa shouted, 'C'marn you two. We are not waiting for ever.'

Monica nudged Pat on the shoulder and Pat had no choice but to retaliate and so nudged her back. Monica hit Pat on the shoulder with her fists, but reluctantly, as if she were merely poking at a snake to see its reaction. Pat swung her arm round and caught Monica on the back. But Monica could not summon up any anger and lightly hit Pat on the shoulder again.

'If you two spend the whole time doing that, then you'll get it from me,' Tresa threatened. Then, as if a volcano had erupted in her head, spewing out all the rage she had been storing up about her father's incarceration, Pat began to swing her fists with the anger and fearlessness of a little demon. Everyone was stunned and the clapping and singing stopped momentarily. Even Tresa was dumbstruck until she remembered the occasion and went around the ring railing at everyone to sing and clap. Pat was raining blows on Monica, who put her hands up to protect her face.

'OK, Pat,' Tresa said walking up to the two girls. 'You're the winner.'

But Pat did not hear her and continued to hit Monica until Tresa summoned her cronies to hold her down. She then told Monica to hit Pat while Pat was being restrained, but Monica walked away, broke through the ring and headed for the mulberry trees, where she sat down against a tree and cried. To everyone's surprise Pat ran after Monica and sat down, placing her arm around Monica's shoulder. They were both crying. I wanted to join them and comfort them both, but I did not have the courage. Tresa was taken aback and ordered us all to disperse.

Everyone was afraid of Tresa and would not dare to object to or tell Sister what was going on. If they did, they would be waylaid by the bully and her followers somewhere in the school, or out in the bush where we went for walks, and beaten. Priscilla once let slip to the Sister in charge that there were girls fighting. Sister walked over to the ring only to find two girls holding hands and swinging each other around while the clapping and singing continued.

'Who is fighting?' Sister asked

'Fighting, Sister? No one is fighting,' said Tresa. 'We're

having a competition to see which two girls can swing the fastest.'

Placated, Sister returned to her base.

Poor Priscilla. Her life was made such a misery that she began routinely to run away, until one day she actually made it back to Northern Rhodesia (Zambia), never to be seen in the school again.

Thirteen

At the end of the first week of the holidays, I was still at the school. The nuns did their best to keep those of us who were not going anywhere entertained, and on the Saturday they took us to a fair in Bulawayo. Our little group walked around, chaperoned by one of the nuns. We walked among the stalls, fascinated by the colourful wares on display but none of us with the money to buy anything. We watched jugglers and clowns and other performers. There was a fashion show, and I was mildly shocked by women showing themselves off and swaying their bodies in what seemed to me to be a wickedly suggestive way. I nudged one of the girls.

'Do you think we should be looking at this?'

We both looked at the nun, but she was engrossed in the catwalk and unconcerned. Then she hurried us along to an open space where people were beginning to gather. She found a spot, where we sat down on the ground and she stood behind us. More people gathered. Suddenly there was a loud beating of drums and a group of black men, carrying spears and shields, naked to the waist, their muscular chests shining with oil, stamped and swayed into the empty space in front of us. They wore skirts of feathers and animal tails over their shorts, and ostrich feathers on their heads, stretching their necks upwards like ostriches. I sat in the front row directly in front of the dancers. The men continued their dance, swaying their bodies rhythmically as if they were stalking an animal, jerking and thrusting their spears upwards and fiercely stamping their feet in unison as they sang. The drums rolled with caution, with tension and then with joy. I was enjoying the performance when suddenly the men let out a collective shout, simultaneously thrusting their spears forward and stamping hard on the ground. A rivulet of terror ran through me and I screamed, stood up and ran to hide behind the nun. A few people laughed. None of the other children seemed concerned. Perhaps they had seen it all before.

'Don't be stupid, Maud. Sit down. It's only a dance,' Sister said. But I refused to budge and slowly crept to the back of the crowd. I stayed there until the dance ended and it was time for us to move on. I had seen another girl, Florrie, give a jump when the dancers shouted and lunged forward, but Florrie had not run away.

'Weren't you scared of those men, Florrie?' I asked later, hoping that in Florrie I might find a kindred soul and not feel so stupid.

'No, it was just the Machanganis. That's how they dance,' said Florrie.

'But I saw you get a shock, just like me,' I insisted.

'Yah, but I wasn't scared. They were only dancing, isn't it?'

Not for the first time, I felt a complete idiot. I wondered if I would always go through life making silly blunders like this. Both the Ndebele and the Shangaan people who Florrie referred to as the Machanganis moved north to Zimbabwe and Mozambique from South Africa during the reign of Chaka, the Zulu king, in the nineteenth century. The

Shangaans, who lived in the south-east of the country, were well known for their dancing though the dancers on this occasion were more likely to have been Amandebele as they lived in the Bulawayo area.

But why did I have to be so timid and why would I be afraid of a group of African men dancing? Had I seen this dance at home in my mother's village I would not have been afraid, so why now? On reflection, I can think of two possible explanations. Firstly, this was Matabeleland, a part of the country where the Amandebele lived and were reputed to be tougher and fiercer than the Shona. In my childlike way I may have thought that their fierce dance was surely evidence of this. The second and better explanation might be that in my head I had separated African men who came from my mother's village and who I knew to be kind, caring people, from African men I did not know who, in my child's mind, could have been the kind who stole children and sold them to witch doctors for medicine. I had not, in any case, ever seen this kind of dance and I had felt particularly vulnerable sitting in the front.

On Monday morning, some of the girls were wandering around listlessly and grumbled to Sister Frances that they were bored. I was not bored. I had a hobby. If I was not reading, I was pasting pictures in scrapbooks. I was hooked on Enid Blyton and was also an avid reader of *Judy* and *Bunty* comics. I had developed a fascination for ballet (it took me a while to realise that I had to say 'ball*ay*' and not 'ball*ett*'), which always featured in the comic books. I spent hours cutting out and sticking pictures of ballerinas, drawing elaborate designs around pictures of Anna Pavlova and Margot Fonteyn, who were regular heroines in the stories. The nuns seemed to have got caught up in my passion and kept me supplied with books about ballet or about my favourite ballerinas. One day Sister Frances handed me a pair of ballet shoes. I pranced around on

the tips of my toes, never having seen a ballet actually performed and therefore having no idea what I was supposed to
do other than stand on my tiptoes, like they did in the comics,
and try to lift my legs. When I asked Sister Frances if I could
learn how to do ballet, she seemed amused and, shaking her
head, she told me that ballet was only for Europeans. By the
time I got to secondary school in Salisbury, I had torn up my
scrapbooks and given up on ballet. For the time being, however, ballet and Enid Blyton's Malory Towers absorbed my
waking hours.

Sister Frances was at her wits' end trying to keep the
other girls entertained when she came up with the curious
notion that we should sit in the playground in front of the
dormitory and loosen up the coir that had gone lumpy in the
mattresses. I asked Sister if I could continue with my scrap-
book, but she replied that it would not be fair on the others.
We complained, but she insisted that 'the devil makes use of
idle hands' and so, moaning and dragging our feet, we sat in
a circle on the ground around three mattresses, two girls to
each mattress, and began to take their guts apart. I was particularly annoyed that I too had to join in.

We talked about what we wanted to do when we had
completed secondary school while we ripped the intestines
mercilessly out of the mattresses.

'I'm going to be a nurse,' said Florrie. Florrie was the
youngest among us and brainy. She was the classic foundling
who, the rumour went, had been placed at the door of the
cathedral in Salisbury. She was therefore raised by the nuns
from birth. She and Alice were the only genuine orphans I
knew among the girls in the school in having no known
parents.

'I'm going to go overseas,' Esther said. Esther, like me,
had spent her early years in a village with her mother. She
had no siblings, and when her mother died when she was five

years old, she had been looked after by her grandfather, who had found the task of raising a little girl too difficult. He had taken the child to the local mission school and asked for help, and Esther ended up at Bushtick.

'I'm going to look after children,' said Winnie, who had special needs and only ever played with children that were much younger than her. Winnie became quite agitated whenever she had to say something to anyone but little children. She had a wide grin on her face and her eyes had a look of surprise, as if even she was not sure that the voice that spoke was hers. Everyone – that is, all the children – loved Winnie, who was as gentle as a saint and whose life was made a misery by the maids because of her constant bed-wetting. Bernadette was her younger sister, though because of Winnie's special needs, she was generally regarded as the older sister and Winnie's protector.

Alice was pretty, with large, dark brown eyes, full, shapely lips and long brown ringlets envied by those of us with difficult-to-manage frizzy hair. Her mother I understood to have been a white girl who had spent her pregnancy in a home for unmarried girls in Bulawayo. Her father, it was believed, was an African man who had been employed by the girl's family.

'I'm going to get married and have a big house in Barham Green for my children, and my husband is going to be a teacher and we'll go to South Africa on holiday, and Salisbury, and other places,' said Alice.

Barham Green! The very name sounded exotic. I tried to imagine what it would be like to live in a Coloured area like Barham Green and go on holiday with my husband and children to South Africa. Little did I know that at this time, in the late 1950s and early 1960s, life was a struggle for many residents of Barham Green, the first area in Bulawayo to be set aside for Coloured people. With more Coloured people moving into the big cities during the Federation years, there was a tight squeeze on accommodation and some people lived in squalid conditions. I had been lost in my little day-dream when I realised that everyone was looking at me. I looked up, and instead of carrying on the narrative about the future I said, 'My sister is here.'

They stared at me, sure that my mind was no longer properly hinged.

'We want to know what you're going to do when you finish school,' Esther said impatiently.

'But my sister is here,' I insisted, and began to dust the coir strands off my lap and prepare to stand up.

'You just want to bunk,' said Bernadette. 'We're gonna tell Sister.'

The boarding house was L-shaped, with the longest part of the L housing the dormitory. It hid from our view the sec-tion of the school which had the office, the visitors' centre, the dining room and the gate into the school. They knew that there was no way that I could have seen my sister arriving, and yet as I sat there, I had had a clear vision of my sister Margie entering the school gate. I stood up just as Sister Frances appeared through the door with Sisi Margie follow-ing behind her. I began to walk towards them even before Sister had called me, and I heard one of the girls whisper, 'She's a witch.'

Sister Frances told Sisi Margie that we would have to leave the next day, when the driver could take us to Bula-wayo. That evening Sisi Margie had her meal with us in the dining room and then joined me and the other girls as we sat under the mulberry trees and chatted before bedtime. I intro-duced her to the girls as 'Sisi Margie', as she was my older sister and it was the height of bad manners to refer to some-one older by name alone. Sisi Margie brought sweets, biscuits and fruit for us to share. Later, Sister Frances told her to take the bed next to me in the near-empty dormitory. I had been self-conscious at first and worried that someone would call her a nanny, but the other girls took her presence in their stride, except on one occasion when someone asked, 'Is she your stepsister?' I nodded. I was not yet acquainted with the term 'step-' or 'half-sister' and would not be until I was in secondary school.

Bernadette said to Sisi Margie, 'Did you phone the Sisters to tell them you were coming to fetch Maud?'

'Oh no, I have no telephone,' Sisi Margie replied.

'So how did Maud know you were coming?'

Sisi Margie's knitted eyebrows turned in my direction.

I shrugged. 'I don't know,' I said. 'I just felt it.'

This was the first of several such telepathic connections that I had with my sister, and that visit was one of the things that Sisi Margie and I reminisced about many years later in the weeks before she died.

Fourteen

Sisi Margie had new employers. They had two daughters. On the first day after our arrival, Sisi Margie had gone to work early and I woke up to the sounds of children talking and laughing. I climbed out of the child's cot where I had spent an uncomfortable night with my skinny legs poking out between the bars at the end. I had not wanted to sleep alone in the kitchen and the only other choice was the cot, long since vacated by Margie's youngest child, who now lived with her paternal grandmother in a village. This was because there were severe restrictions on the lives of black workers who stayed in the city. Sisi Margie, however, was sure that her previous employers had forbidden children because they did not want children to distract her from total devotion to their needs. She was nevertheless quite happy to relinquish her responsibility for her children to their grandmothers, arguing truthfully that in the Shona culture it was traditional for grandparents to raise their grandchildren.

I peeped around the corner of Sisi Margie's little house and there were two white girls in the garden. I stood and watched them discreetly while I ate the doughnut and drank the cup of milk that Sisi Margie had left for me. One girl looked about twelve years old, my age, and the other was about eight or nine. I was too shy to go out until Sisi Margie came and took me to see them.

During my stay Mrs Stewart, the girls' mother and Sisi Margie's employer, was extremely kind to me. She insisted that I have my lunches with her children and when she learnt about the cot that I slept in, she offered Sisi Margie a bed for me in the house. But Sisi Margie declined, and so Mrs Stewart suggested she put the cot mattress on the floor and augment it with cushions and extra blankets. All this was most unusual. Europeans did not usually invite the relatives of their servants to play with their children, let alone to sleep in the house. It may be that Mrs Stewart was motivated by the fact that I was a Coloured and not an African, and that she knew that I was being raised by European nuns and had grown accustomed to sleeping in a bed. She may also have disagreed with the politics of the country, as not long after I met them, they moved back to England. The main motivation, however, would certainly have been kindness. She did not have to do any of this, whatever her beliefs. Her daughters, Lucy and Jackie, were equally open and inviting, and we became firm friends immediately and spent a lot of time together, including playing with their friends who lived next door.

One day Lucy invited me to go swimming with them at the public pool.

I carried a little bag with a costume that Mrs Stewart gave me and a towel.

When we arrived, I could hear shouting, squealing and splashing water. I felt apprehensive but certain that with Lucy and Jackie there, all would be fine.

At the entrance, Lucy took some money out of her bag and said, 'Three please,' to the man in the booth. He looked at her, at Jackie and then at me and paused.

'Is the third one for her?' he asked, his eyes not leaving my face.

'Yes,' said Lucy.

'She can't come in here,' he said, pursing his lips and staring at Lucy.

'Why not?' asked Lucy

'Because she is a Coloured and this swimming pool is for Europeans only,' the man replied with impatience. Lucy turned around and looked at me, puzzled, as if she had not realised it until that moment. She turned back to look at the man.

'But she is almost my colour,' she protested.

'I will give you two tickets. She,' he said, pointing his finger at me, 'cannot come in. She can wait outside for you if she wants. But there are people waiting to go in, so make up your mind.'

Lucy continued to stare at the man as if unsure that she had heard him correctly.

'Do you want to come in or not?' the man snapped.

Lucy took the money off the counter saying, 'Let's go home. Come, Maud,' and we walked out with several pairs of eyes boring into my face and back. I walked silently alongside Lucy, who looked contemplative, while Jackie, clearly not understanding what had just happened, complained.

'But Lucy, I want to go swimming. Why can't we go?' she whined.

'Because,' Lucy said.

'Because what?' Jackie asked in frustration.

'Just shut up, Jackie.'

The Coloured community at that time had been protesting about the segregated swimming for some time. This eventually led to a repeal of the law, and Coloureds were then allowed to use the same swimming pools as white people. Africans were still prohibited.

Fifteen

I spent about nine days altogether with Sisi Margie. The day after the pool incident, she bought herself a brand-new bike, which she allowed me to use. It was a shiny metallic green, with a bell, a small basket and a carrier. Salaries for domestic servants were so low that the only way they could afford luxury or new items was through a system of micro-banking: a collective was formed and each individual gave a portion of their wages to someone who took the position of banker, and each month the total amount was given to one of the people in the group for those purchases that would otherwise have been out of their reach. Lucy dedicated her time to teaching me how to ride. Sisi Margie's husband also spent time running up and down the alleyway holding onto the back of the bike until eventually I was riding alone and only realised it when I heard him shouting, 'You can come back now.'

It was time for me to spend a few days with Amaiguru Hilda in Marandellas. My oldest sister, Filida, came to fetch me. Like Sisi Margie, she was tall and slim. She was twenty-three years old and had recently joined a religious sect which had been founded in 1953 by Alice Lenshina, a charismatic woman from Northern Rhodesia (Zambia). Lenshina and her followers were persecuted in Zambia, but branches of the sect appeared in different places, including Rhodesia and exist in Zimbabwe to this day.

That Sunday I said goodbye to Lucy and Jackie. We hugged each other while Sisi Margie and Mrs Stewart looked on. Lucy and I promised to write to each other, which we did even after she and her family had gone back to England. Eventually I lost Lucy's address and the correspondence came to an end.

I pleaded with Sisi Margie to let me ride her bike to the bus station, hanging on to her, repeating 'please' 'please', until she finally gave in. Sisi Filida and Sisi Margie were walking together, absorbed in catching up after a long time of not seeing each other while I rode the bike ahead of them. Sisi Filida glided along like a sylph while Sisi Margie walked with her characteristic heavy tread, which added a bounce to her walk as if she had springs tacked to her feet, giving the impression that she was moving fast, but in fact she was making little progress. At some point on the journey we crossed a large piece of scrubland which lay between a residential area and an industrial site. The grass was short and patchy and paths criss-crossed the almost-bare land in every direction. Bits of plastic and newspaper stuck to the low, leafless shrubs that were barely surviving the onslaught of human feet and dog waste. A railway line, used only for goods trains, ran east to west along the northern edge of the scrub towards the industrial site. The path we were on ran south to north, meeting the railway line on the northern edge of the scrub before disappearing into a scattering of eucalyptus trees on its way to a township and the bus station.

'Make sure you stop and wait for us when you arrive at the railway line,' Sisi Filida cautioned me.

I rode as fast as I could, enjoying the vastness of the blue sky and the freedom of the open scrub. The only other people were a man and a woman who were ahead of me and would have crossed into the woodland by the time I arrived at the railway line. I got there well ahead of my sisters and got off the bike. At that moment a goods train came idling around the bend looking for all the world like a *chongololo* or millipede puffing on a cigarette. I loved the sound of trains; they reminded me of exciting journeys to and from school. I stared at the smoke billowing from the engine and then at the great pumping iron pistons. I had never been this close to a moving train, unless I was inside it as a passenger, and my eyes were riveted to the wheels. I wondered what it was that made that rhythmic clickety-clack sound. As the train went past, I shifted my gaze from the wheels to the engine driver's cabin – and froze. Standing by the window was a boy of about fourteen or fifteen with his head cocked to one side and pointing what looked like a long stick at me. My heart felt like it was contracting, I could barely breathe; I felt the blood draining out of my face and sweat on the palms of my hands. I clung to the handlebars of the bicycle as if they were crutches. I turned my head slowly to see where my sisters were. They were absorbed in their talk and too far away to see what was happening. The moment seemed to last forever while the boy held the rifle pointing directly at me, turning as the train went past to keep me in his sights. I was paralysed with fear and concerned that if I tried to run away, that would merely provoke him to shoot. I had heard, either on the childhood grapevine or in the mystical whisperings of adults in sombre village kitchens, that white people could kill black people for no reason whatsoever and nothing would happen, not even an inquiry into the incident. I stared at the boy, certain that I was going to die, because in this place, I thought, no one would know what had happened. I stayed rooted to the spot even as the last of the carriages disappeared into the distance.

'Why aren't you riding your bike? Did you fall or have you forgotten how to?' Sisi Margie teased when they saw me standing still, looking like a statue that had taken root.

I looked at them. 'There was a boy in that train. He was pointing a gun at me.'

'Was he?' said Sisi Filida. They looked at each other. Then Sisi Margie laughed and said, 'He was just playing, showing off that he had a gun and wanted to see if he could frighten you. Come, let's go.'

Sixteen

Little had changed in the two years since I had last stayed at Amaiguru Hilda's, except that I noticed that Pamela, Mr Shiri's daughter, now helped more with the household chores. Morsia, however, still bore the brunt of the work. I was also roped into various tasks, including going with Morsia to the bus station to sell *vetkoeks*, deep-fried sweet doughy cakes, to travellers. For some reason I was not as bothered about doing this as I had been about selling mangoes with Stan. I was not sure why. Perhaps it was because I was older and selling exclusively to black people. Why this should have made it easier for me, I cannot tell. Was it because black people knew what it was like to make a living in the most menial of ways and so were less likely to sneer and be judgmental? Or could it be that I was more worried about what white people thought about me than black people? It could be that I was just more comfortable with black people than I was with white people. Morsia and I enjoyed the walk to town alone and there was a sense of achievement when we returned with empty baskets and money in our pockets.

Amaiguru Hilda had not changed much either. She still

worked for the Greek family in the centre of town. She was never late for work and always started at 6 a.m., her green maid's uniform spotless and thoroughly ironed every morning and her hat, perched on her head like a nurse's hat, carefully starched. In the evenings after we had washed the dishes and tidied up – a big shift from the previous culture when Morsia had done most of the work – Amaiguru gathered us together, calling '*ela, ela*' in the manner of her Greek employer. Amaiguru had picked up a smattering of Greek and used what she knew so liberally and with such bravado that it never occurred to any of us that she might have been making up some of the words as she went along. Years later I discovered that the only word she used correctly was *ela* (come on). She nearly always followed this with *ti kanis* (how are you?), but in a context and tone of voice that made us think it meant hurry up. Another of her favourite words was *orYste* ('I'm sorry' – said if you didn't hear something), but it was always used by Amaiguru Hilda as a reprimand!

It was a significant time in the history of Rhodesia. An African liberation movement was growing, not only in numerical strength but in making greater and more urgent demands on the government. The movement was not being taken seriously by the government, as there was a belief that African people did not have the capability to launch a serious challenge to the status quo. The African National Congress in South Africa had, after all, existed for much longer and without achieving its political goals.

In 1959 the government passed the Unlawful Organisations Act, which specified that there were to be no meetings during weekends and public holidays – the only time that African people in urban areas had the time to themselves – and the Preventive Detention Act. These were followed in 1960 by the Law and Order (Maintenance) Act (LOMA), which was so restrictive and punitive that even the right-wing Chief Justice of the Federation, Sir Robert Tredgold, described it as 'an anthology of horrors' and resigned his position in protest. The human rights lawyer Reginald Austin, in his report to UNESCO in 1975, described LOMA as 'a system of authoritarian government as inhumane if not as savage as any dictatorship existing', and it was directed almost exclusively against people of colour.

This was the period of the Federation, an alliance of three British territories – Northern Rhodesia (Zambia), Nyasaland (Malawi) and Southern Rhodesia. The white Rhodesian government under the leadership of Sir Winston Field had been campaigning for the independence of Rhodesia under white rule, or 'civilised government', as they termed it. The Rhodesian government tried to introduce a few liberal concessions in order to bring African people onside in an attempt to win British approval of independence. The constitution of 1961 offered minimal representation of Africans in the Senate and made some surface efforts at desegregation. African views were not sought, and Joshua Nkomo and members of the Zimbabwe African People's Union (ZAPU) saw the constitution for what it was – a bid to appease them in order to get the approval of the British for what in effect would lead to an entrenchment of white privilege at the expense of the black majority. They rejected the half-hearted measures that were proposed and refused to cooperate, instead holding meetings around the country to mobilise the people. The response of the government was to institute the most authoritarian and punitive laws to date, what Austin, in his report, described as 'a classic example of post-modern persecution'. Then in 1962, ZAPU was banned. Amaiguru Hilda was a passionate and active member of ZAPU. She never ceased to talk about liberation and was clearly keen that I should align myself with the African cause. Unlike the previous time I had stayed with her, she had decided that this time I needed to be schooled in tradition.

She now made a point of speaking to me mainly in Shona and explaining the customs and traditions of the Shona people. When a neighbour came by and I went forward to shake her hand, Amaiguru exclaimed, 'Ah! That's not how we do it. Morsi, show her how it's done.'

I watched Morsia extend her right hand with her left hand touching the right elbow and doing a little curtsy.

'That's how we show respect to our elders,' Amaiguru pointed out. When she asked me something and I responded in English, she made me repeat it in Shona, correcting my grammar mistakes. Although I was initially embarrassed, I was no longer afraid to speak Shona and was glad to be able to show off how well I could speak.

Amaiguru did not teach Albert and Pamela tsika. They had come from Malawi with their father and spoke Chinyanja and had their own customs, which were never discussed. They seemed quite wild to me, but Amaiguru did little to rein them in. Albert was twelve like me, Pamela was ten. I liked them and they treated Morsia, who was eight, with kindness. Unfortunately, my sojourns at Amaiguru Hilda's seldom lasted more than a week and I never got to know or form a lasting relationship with Albert and Pamela. Their father worked long, unsocial hours and we rarely saw him, but I envied them the fact that they did have a father. That was until an incident caused me to question for the first time the role of a father and I was grateful that I did not live permanently with Amaiguru.

One day Mr Shiri sent for us to come to the hotel where he worked and collect some food and cakes that he had especially kept aside for us. Going to the hotel as his guests was a rare privilege, and we laughed and smiled and thumped each other's backs or clapped each other's hands. Amaiguru told us to wash the dust off our legs, which looked as if we had been wading in chalk, and to change our clothes for cleaner ones. Morsia hung back, unsure if this privilege extended to her, so I took her hand and led her into the bedroom to change. There was no sound from Amaiguru and even Morsia managed a smile as she put on a dress that I had outgrown. But just as we were about to leave we heard the familiar call.

'Morsi, I need you to stay behind.'

Morsia's face fell and there was such sadness in her eyes that my heart felt like it would crack open. I was afraid and expecting a sharp reproach when I went to Amaiguru and said, 'Amai, please can I stay with Morsia?'

Amaiguru Hilda looked at me, surprised, and whether she was pleased with this show of magnanimity or merely taken aback, she said, 'Well, my girl, you can all go. But I have some chores for Morsi which she can do later.'

Morsia and I whooped with joy and, holding hands, we joined Albert and Pamela. When we returned later that evening, Amaiguru seemed to have forgotten all about the chores.

At the hotel, Mr Shiri, with his watery eyes, his little goatee and his developing paunch, took us down a few steps into a large kitchen where he gave us cakes and soft drinks. The Matombo Hotel was the best known and perhaps the only hotel in town. We all felt privileged and lucky to have such an important person in our family. He took two small baskets, which had been tied with large cloths to keep the contents safe, and handed one to Albert and one to me, saying, 'You two older ones are responsible for making sure this gets home safely. You understand?'

We nodded and started to make our way up the stairs.

'Albert,' Mr Shiri said, stopping us in our tracks, 'take the two girls upstairs with you and wait at the entrance. Maud, you come back here for a minute.'

I followed him into a room that felt cold and had shelves stacked with various food items. He walked to the back of the room and stopped in front of a large fridge. Then, making as if to open the door, he suddenly took the basket out of my hands, placed it on the floor and, grabbing me by my shoulders, planted a kiss full on my lips. I felt nauseated but was so stunned that I stood there staring at the floor as if something had hit me on the head and made me lose all thought and direction. For years afterwards I associated a man's kiss with the smell of onions. There was a sound coming from the kitchen. Mr Shiri opened the fridge door pretending to be looking for something and in a loud voice said, 'Make sure you don't run and play on the way home, otherwise you will arrive without any food. OK?' Then he whispered conspiratorially, 'Bring the baskets back tomorrow and I will have something very special for you. But don't come with the others. I will tell Mother to send you on your own.'

I knew that I could not tell the others – this was Albert and Pamela's father, after all. I could not tell Amaiguru Hilda either. Mr Shiri was her husband and she would never have believed me. Did he do this to Pamela and to Morsia? Was this what having a father was about? I did not think so. My experiences in the village had never led me to this conclusion, even with men who were not in a father or caretaker role. On the way home I was silent and barely heard what the others were talking about, let alone took part in the laughter and games.

'What's wrong?' Albert asked.

'I think I had too much cake. I feel sick,' I said, and retreated into my confusion.

That evening when Amaiguru got home from work, she told us that Baba was not coming home that night and would be staying at the hotel. I felt such a deep sense of relief that my mood lifted and I took full part in the chatter and laughter.

After dinner Amaiguru asked me to help her move the beds around in her bedroom. There were two single beds which were pushed together. We separated them, pushing each one against the wall on either side of the room. I felt so light-hearted and gay that I put all my energy into helping.

'You can sleep in here tonight,' she said. I would rather have slept with the others, even though we shared two to a bed, but Amaiguru presented it as a great privilege, and I did not argue.

That night I was sleeping deeply when I was half awakened by someone's hand stroking my thigh. There was a pungent odour of alcohol. The hand was trying to pull my pyjamas down. I stiffened, now wide awake. Then an arm went over my waist, pulling me backwards. Terrified, I cried out loudly, pushed the hand away and jumped out of the bed. Amaiguru, who was in the other bed, moved slightly but did not get up.

'Amai,' I whispered tearfully, 'there is someone in my bed.'

'OK, go and sleep with the others,' she said without looking at me or lifting her head. I ran the short distance to the children's bedroom and climbed in with Morsia. I slept fitfully and by the time we all woke up the next morning, Mr Shiri had gone to work. I had already determined that if I were to be sent to the hotel, I would cry and Amaiguru would have to desist. She did not mention the hotel. Before she left for work, I approached her tentatively and asked her if I could go home to the village that day. She laughed.

'And how will you get there?' she asked.

I looked at her, realising the stupidity of my request.

'Look,' she said, 'it's Saturday today. Tomorrow we will go to church and on Monday I will put you on a bus. So not long now.' And with that she picked up her handbag and left the house.

The following day, Sunday, Mr Shiri took Albert and Pamela somewhere and Amaiguru told Morsia and me to dress in our smartest clothes as we were going with her to the United Methodist Church, where she was a member. She donned her uniform of a black skirt, a red blouse with a large white collar, a white, sailor-like hat, and flat black shoes.

I was thoroughly enjoying the service. There was joy in people's voices as they clapped to the rhythm of the song, some swaying their shoulders in a dance and moving their fists to the beat. I looked over towards Morsia, who was on the other side of Amaiguru and who was clapping her hands and singing, her face relaxed and her eyes shining. I wished I knew the words too so that I could join in. I liked singing and was in the church choir at school. But I felt guilty and feared that I may have been committing a sin by attending a heretic service. I was ruminating on the time that I would have to spend in Purgatory when my hand was suddenly seized by Amaiguru and she marched Morsia and me to the front of the congregation. Eyes looked back at us from a sea of khaki, and red, black and white. A baby called out from the back but otherwise all else was still. Amaiguru closed her eyes and said a short prayer in a soft voice filled with gentle emotion, asking God to acknowledge the presence of his children and to bless everyone present. She cleared her throat and began to preach in a lucid, loud voice, articulating each Shona word with care. I stood there fidgeting and wondering what I was supposed to do.

'My dear brothers and sisters, do we agree that God created us all equal and in his image?' Amaiguru Hilda asked, in a voice that was measured and direct as if she were merely asking if the milkman had arrived.

There was a general chorus of 'Yes, sister', and 'Of course', and some clapping.

She continued in the same voice. 'Then why are we black people at the bottom of the heap? Is that what God wants?'

'No!' the congregation replied vehemently.

Then, as if lifted up by the passion of her fellow worshippers, Amaiguru raised her voice, and with animated conviction she asked, 'Do you think God is happy that our political leaders are called terrorists, our political parties are harassed and banned by law when they are the only means we have of expressing our grievances?'

An angry chorus of 'No' followed.

Amaiguru took hold of Morsia's and my hands and raised them in the air.

'See these children. Are they the same colour?'

'No,' shouted the congregation. One or two people giggled.

Amaiguru paused and looked around at the faces.

'No,' she said with fervour, 'but they are both my children. Does it mean that because one is the child of a white man and is a different colour from her sister, I should treat them differently?'

'No,' came the emphatic chorus.

'No,' echoed Amaiguru in a low voice. She paused to allow the 'No' to travel to each heart and sink deeply and irretrievably. Then, raising her voice again and looking up into the rafters as if to look into the eyes of the God she spoke of, she said, 'It would be a sin in the eyes of God if I treated one well and treated the other badly. Yet that is what God sees every day. God sees his white children given everything of the best and sees his black children treated worse than the white people treat their dogs. We are treated like slaves, even. We are given no respect and no dignity.' Amaiguru paused and looked around. Her voice laden with feeling, she said, '*Mwari Anochema, Anotichemera isu, vana vake* (God weeps, God weeps for us his children).'

The congregation was riveted. Amaiguru Hilda was a dynamic and charismatic speaker. She outlined the inhumanity of forcibly removing Africans from their homes and their productive agricultural land and relocating them to poor, unproductive parts of the country. She spoke emotionally about the lack of educational opportunities that stymied any attempts by Africans to improve their lives economically and condemned them to perpetual servitude. She was angry about the daily humiliations of the 'Pass' laws, which meant African adults had to carry an identity card at all times as they could be stopped at any time and asked to produce it. This was mainly relevant in the towns and cities but they had to be carried in the rural areas too, especially during the politically unstable period; the insulting language with which whites, including children, addressed African people, regardless of age or status; the degradations of being a third-class citizen without real citizenship rights in one's own country; the inferior housing; the lack of facilities; and, importantly, the conditions that severely limited Africans' right to vote. There was no route by which African people could represent their own interests instead of having their interests defined by the white government.

'I, like most of us here, did not have a high-school education,' she said quietly. 'Do you think that makes me too stupid to know what is good for me?' A few people shouted 'No' and there was a low grumble like a warning growl among the congregation. Amaiguru continued. 'Do we need the white man to tell us whether we are happy or not? And yet that is exactly what the prime minister tells the world – that we, the African people, are happy. So if we are so happy, why are they banning our political parties and putting our leaders in prison?' Amaiguru continued in this vein, her voice rising and falling, her body language tense and angry. When she had finished, the whole congregation stood up and clapped. I realised that this was no ordinary church service. There was something deep and far-reaching going on in the hearts and minds not just of the people present, but also throughout the country. I now made sense of the time that leaflets came raining down on the school playground and Sister Dolores, picking one up, shouted exultantly, 'Alleluia, God be praised. The government has banned the terrorists, and now we can have peace. Alleluia.'

None of the children at school had understood who or what she was talking about. I now appreciated Amaiguru Hilda's determination that I should learn the language, traditions and customs of my people – as she never ceased to remind me. I understood about injustice. I saw it in the kind of homes that Africans lived in compared with the luxury of white people's houses. I particularly felt it at school when my mother was made to sleep in the laundry, despite the fact that there was room in the visitors' centre. I saw it and felt it in so many ways, but until now I had never given it a name or questioned its normality. To my surprise, I found myself lifted up and carried along with the tide of passion and, not knowing most of the words of the hymns, I joined in the choruses with the voices that were raised with even more energy and feeling than they'd had before, clapping my hands vigorously along with the singing.

Ndoda, Ndoda, Ndoda Mwari muyamuri
Uri wangu
Ndakatengwa neropa raishe
Ndawa wake chose.

I love God who is my saviour
You are mine
I was bought with the blood of the Lord
I am his for ever.

Something profound took place inside of me as I realised that what was going on in this church was not only about prayer but about freedom. I looked up at Amaiguru Hilda with awe.

After the service, Amaiguru did not take us home but into town. She led us down some steps and knocked on a door to a basement below a shoe shop. There was a long pause before a diminutive man with a thick neck, small eyes and grey hair opened the door a crack and peeped suspiciously out. We were told to enter quickly, and the door was shut and locked behind us.

The room was empty except for a table and four chairs in the centre, where there was a man sitting, seemingly doodling on a pad of paper. He was a stout man, entirely bald but sporting a thick bushy beard. When he saw who had entered, he said loudly, 'It's OK. You can come out. It's our sister.' A man emerged from a door at the back of the room. The door had the same wallpaper covering it as the wall. I stared wide-eyed when I saw it open as if by magic. He was a handsome man, tall, clean-shaven and smartly dressed in a grey suit and blue open-necked shirt. I recognised him at once as Joseph, my cousin's fiancé. The men shook hands with Amaiguru and were pleased to see her. Then they shook hands with Morsia and me. I followed Morsia's example and did a little curtsy. The short man who had opened the door looked bemused.

Joseph, with his dark intelligent eyes, looked at Morsia and me. 'But Amai, why the children?' he asked.

'They will be fine. I needed them in church today.' They nodded. Suddenly the two men were moving the table, removing a rug on which it stood, and opening a trapdoor set in the floor. The short man reached into the hole and passed boxes and a mysterious metal contraption out to the others. They set up the contraption and began operating it.

It was a crude but effective printing press that churned out lots of paper, which they collected, cut, and packed in boxes. I saw the word ZAPU in large letters on the pieces of paper. The rest was in Shona, which at that time I could not read. Amaiguru told Morsia and me to take a bun and a Coke each, and when we had finished eating, we were to help pack the boxes.

I listened intently to the conversation between the adults. I discovered that George, an important member of ZAPU, was Joseph's uncle, and that Joseph himself was a local leader and needed to 'disappear' to Zambia. Morsia and I were asked not to talk to anyone – not even Albert and Pamela – about what we had witnessed that day because Amaiguru would be locked up, tortured and killed by the government secret service if they found out. I could not fully understand the talk of intrigues and conspiracies, the need to flee, the capture of certain people, the complex as well as corrupt machinations of politics, but I knew with certainty that something fundamental was changing in the country. Much of the adult conversation made no sense to me, but I did catch one phrase among the many things Amaiguru talked about that left me puzzled and confused. It was not until I was at university that I realised what she had meant when she said, '. . . and the Coloureds will be the first to go.' Many years later, after Zimbabwe had gained independence and President Robert Mugabe was in the driving seat, he made a statement that transported me right back to that basement and Amaiguru Hilda. 'As for you Coloureds,' he said, 'your fathers were not indigenous to Zimbabwe. You can go to England where your fathers came from.' I was glad that at age twelve I had been blissfully unaware that I was innocently packing leaflets that gave out the message that I and others like me were in the enemy's camp. I was aware, at a visceral level, of the middle position occupied by

Coloured and Asian people but unaware of the resentment among Africans at this privilege, which was based entirely on perceptions of race. At the time, I felt confused. Was I included in Amaiguru's understanding of Coloured, and where did she want us to go? I felt that she could not possibly be including me because of all the effort she was making to teach me African customs. I realised later – and with horror – that not only was I inevitably included, but that Amaiguru had not meant to banish us from the country at all. She had envisioned an even worse fate for Coloureds than Mugabe – death. I was puzzled and conflicted because Amaiguru had always cared well for me and showed me a great deal of affection.

There were, of course, good reasons for African resentment of Coloureds. The whole ideology of separate development was based on how closely one was connected to white people by dint of skin colour. Colour of skin was a passport to opportunity or a passport to servitude. If a Coloured woman had a child with a white man, that child had infinitely better chances in life than the child of a Coloured woman with a black man. Coloured people were given privileges that Africans were deprived of, purely on the basis of our biological connection to white people, and also as a political convenience, when the small number of votes we carried was useful to the white government. We had access to better education, better jobs and higher salaries than Africans. All in all, our prospects were better. But the opportunities given to Coloured people were limited compared to those of whites, and although we were categorised as European in relation to land and education, we were treated with the same arrogance handed down to all people of colour and segregated from whites in nearly all spheres. This did not prevent many Coloured people from assimilating the demeaning and derogatory attitudes of white people towards Africans and developing a separate identity

Amai with Maud at nine months
in Makwiro, April 1951.

Mr Lanning and helper
in Makwiro, April 1951.

Maud, aged fifteen, at a ceremony where students crown a statue of Mary, mother of Jesus, as the 'Queen of May', 1966.

Maud, aged sixteen, in the centre of a row of prefects at St John's school, 1967.

Maud with a friend outside a Europeans Only toilet in Salisbury, *c.* 1971.

Sisi Filida, Maud's eldest sister, at Amai's homestead in Murehwa, *c.* 1972.

The road to Murehwa.

Aunt Hilda in full flow
at Maud's wedding.

Wedding Day, 1973. From left to right:
Rodney, Maud, Amai, Stan.

Family at Maud's wedding. From left to right: Patrick, Margie, Abigail,
Aunt Hilda, Rodney, Maud, Stan, Amai, Morsia, Filida.

An ice-cream man with his bicycle in Harare
(former Salisbury), post-independence Zimbabwe.

From left to right: Joanna, Michael, Mationesa and Uncle
sitting on Grandma Chiraswa's grave, August 1993.

Sisi Margie photographed in Cambridge, c. 2002.

Michael with his wife Didem and their children, from top to bottom: Barnie Tafara, Orton Ali and Ida Maud. Turkey, 2020.

Maud with children and grandchildren in Murewha, 2022.

From left to right: Joanna, Michael, Maud and Mationesa
on Maud's 70th birthday in Cambridge.

infused with the same racist beliefs and attitudes. Yet when the struggle for independence became a reality, many Coloured men, especially those who had been raised in the villages or had attended mission schools for African students, threw in their lot with the African struggle.

Early the following day, before going to work, Amaiguru Hilda took me to the bus station and told me that Stan would be waiting in Murehwa for me. I had no idea where Murehwa was.

'Am I not going to see Amai in Bumburwi?' I asked Amaiguru.

'Your mother lives in Murehwa now,' she replied, and I did not ask for further explanation.

Seventeen

The bus rattled along the dirt road, stopping now and again to let people off and on. The landscape was green and crops were either being or had been harvested, as it was late December. This is one of the hottest months, but is in the rainy season and food is generally plentiful unless there has been a drought. I do not recall any experience of drought during the 1960s.

I managed to doze despite the unrelenting vibration and occasional loud talk or laughter. Suddenly someone was shaking me. It was the woman sitting next to me. The bus had stopped. I looked up and saw a white soldier with a gun on his shoulder roughly ordering everyone off the bus. I followed the other passengers who huddled in groups under the sparse shadow of the *matamba* trees on the side of the road. The green fruit of the matamba hung like large golf balls, bending the branches with their weight. The air was oppressively hot, a sign of rain if not an actual storm. Beyond the trees the heat quivered, blurring and distorting the shape of objects in the distance. There were two soldiers – one white and one black. They ordered the bus driver and the conductor to offload every item from the roof of the bus. A man, desperate to get home, started walking towards the bus to lend a hand, when the white soldier caught him on his shoulder with the butt of the gun. I jumped and a shiver went through me when I heard the crack of the gun on the man's shoulder.

The white soldier, who looked younger than his black companion, swept menacing eyes across the frightened faces. 'Nobody move from here,' he said. I looked down at the ground, moved closer to the person near me and tried to be invisible. The white soldier gestured to the black soldier to stand in a particular position to ensure that no one left the group and then began to question the adults. I realised that I was standing next to a man who seemed old, but with hindsight was probably only in his fifties. The soldier began to question him. I kept my face down and pretended not to listen.

'What's your name?'

'My name is Harto, Baas,' said the man, removing his hat and wiping sweat from his forehead.

'Where is your *situpa*?'

The man, holding his hat in one hand, fumbled in his pocket and produced a well-worn identity card or pass with his photograph on it.

'Where did you get on the bus?' the soldier said, looking at the card and then at the man.

'In Marandellas, Baas.'

'What were you doing in Marandellas?'

'I work in the Central Butchery, Baas. My baas is Mr Phillips. You can ask him. I have his telephone number.'

The soldier ignored this and asked, 'Where are you going?' The soldier knew that the bus was destined for Murehwa, but he asked all the same, clearly enjoying the ability to subdue so many people so much older than himself.

'To Murehwa, Baas.'

'Do you know this man?'

The man looked at the picture in the soldier's hand. He transferred his gaze from the photograph to the hat he was holding and, bending his head slightly to show humility, he shook his head.

'No, Baas. I do not know him.'

'Do you know what will happen to you if you lie to me?' the soldier's aggressive voice warned.

'Yes. Baas. I will go to prison.'

'No, you will not go to prison. You will not go anywhere. Your family will not even know where you have gone. Now look at this picture again. Do you know this man?'

The man peered at the photograph, the worry lines on his forehead showing him to be deep in thought.

'No, Baas. It is the truth. I do not know this man.'

The soldier was about to walk away when, as if he had had a second thought, he said, 'Is she with you?'

I realised that he was referring to me, and I looked up. The old man turned to look at me and shook his head.

'No, Baas. I do not know her.'

The soldier summoned me with his forefinger. I followed him with a hollow feeling in the pit of my stomach and wished I could control the shaking in my legs.

'Where is your luggage?' the soldier said to me in a gentle voice.

I walked over to the bus and looked around. I saw my suitcase and pointed to it. Fear gnawed at my insides and I shivered with tension at the knowledge that Amaiguru Hilda's leaflets were concealed at the bottom of the suitcase. I was to give them to my mother. I felt certain that the man on the photograph that the soldiers were inquiring about must be Joseph, my cousin's fiancé. If they discovered that I was associated with him and the leaflets, they would surely shoot me right there and then. Amaiguru could not possibly have known, or perhaps it had not occurred to her that the bus might be stopped. I started to pray silently, 'Hail Mary full of Grace . . .' The soldier told the conductor to put my suitcase back on the bus and, turning to me, blue eyes searching but kind, he said in his soft voice, 'Who are you travelling with?'

'I'm by myself.'

'Where are you going?'

'I'm going to see my mother in Murehwa.'

Jerking his gun towards the bus the soldier said, 'You can go and sit in the bus.'

I went back to my seat but had difficulty controlling the jitters, which had attacked my right leg. I was the only one given the privilege to go and sit in the bus and even at that age I was aware of the reason – I stood out from the rest. I was almost 'one of them', the murungus, and this was the obvious reward.

The bus was strewn with all manner of flotsam and jetsam discarded by passengers as they hurriedly disembarked when the soldiers ordered us out. I sat by the window and observed the goings-on from my privileged perch. There were other children, some not much older than me, clinging to their mothers. The black soldier was now standing alongside the white soldier and appeared to be interpreting. When the soldiers had finished questioning the passengers, they told them to collect their luggage. The soldiers then made them unpack their bags and boxes, placing each item on the ground. The white soldier poked his gun through some of the items as if he were testing an animal that he was not sure was truly dead. Some he lifted with the muzzle of the gun, like looking at a tapeworm in a laboratory. It was unclear what the soldiers were looking for: anything could have been contraband in these unsettled days. They did not confiscate anything. It was almost mid-afternoon. The sun was fierce as people repacked their belongings, some huddling in the shade of the few trees, women with children and the elderly taking priority. The bus should have been in Murehwa two hours earlier. But the soldiers had all the time in the world. A bus was a welcome distraction from the boredom of endless waiting for commands in this godforsaken part of the country.

No one dared to complain. They went through the ritual with the stoicism of the helpless, women comforting their children, the older ones unable to hide their fear. Finally, the driver and conductor were ordered to return the luggage to the roof of the bus. Several men went forward to help and the other passengers clambered into their seats, silent, the strain palpable on all their faces. The bus started up and was about to move when the white soldier walked in front of the bus and banged on it with his hand, signalling the driver to stop. The conductor opened the door and the soldier climbed in. Slowly he walked along the gangway, looking intently at all the faces. I was afraid of giving away my guilt, so I turned and looked out of the window. Tension and anxiety filled the bus, creasing foreheads and clinging to hunched shoulders. People looked away apprehensively.

'You, and you,' the soldier said to two men. 'You come with me.'

The men followed the soldier, who told the bus driver to go. Several eyes looked with pity at the two men as the bus left them behind, standing silently. Their fate could only be guessed at. There was an uncharacteristic silence in the bus as the driver tried to make up some of the lost time. Fear and anxiety had drained everyone's energy. But it was best to be silent. Discretion was everything. There was no knowing whom you could trust. Half an hour later, the bus pulled into the station at Murehwa. My mother and my brother Stan were waiting for me.

Eighteen

Amai lifted me off my feet and twirled me around, laughing and saying, 'Look at my big girl!'

I did not recognise Stan immediately because he had grown so much. His voice was deep as he said, 'Welcome, Maudie,' hugging me and laughing his familiar chuckle.

'We have been waiting for a very long time,' Stan said. 'But we knew what was happening. The army is always stopping the buses.'

'Where are we going?' I asked Stan.

'We are now living at Hakata, our grandfather's village.

'Why?' I asked.

'Our uncles wanted Amai to come back to her father's home.'

'Why?' I repeated, turning to my mother for an explanation. Amai looked at me and said in Shona, 'These things can't always be explained. They thought I should come back, so I came back.'

'In fact,' Stan cut in speaking in English, 'there are some things that happen which I can't explain very well in English. But it is to do with our ancestors. We believe that some of

147

our ancestors wanted our mother to come back here to live in her father's village.'

'How can that happen if they are dead?' I asked innocently.

'Ah, you see,' Stan sighed. 'That's why it's hard to explain. Do you know what a svikiro is?'

I shook my head.

'That is someone who the ancestors can talk to. They give their messages and their good advice for the family through the svikiro. That is what our Amai is. Maybe one day when your Shona is very good Amai can explain it herself.'

I already knew about the importance of the ancestors and the powerful role they played in the lives of the people. But the limit of my understanding was that you do not do or say anything that might offend them, as disaster could befall you or your family. Sad though I was about it, I understood why Amai had to move from Bumburwi to Murehwa.

We were walking along a dirt road so deeply serrated that the only vehicle, a tractor whose trailer was full to capacity with people, crawled along shaking and juddering like a snail with the jitters. I held my mother's rough hand while Stan carried my suitcase.

It was a long way to Amai's homestead and took longer, as Amai stopped periodically to chat with neighbours along the way. The black sky glared at the earth with a menacing warning, emitting the occasional growl while intermittent flashes of lightning twisted across the sky like a rebuke. 'I am going to run home because if the rain comes it will damage your suitcase,' Stan said. We watched him pick up speed, the case forcing him to tilt lopsidedly like a wounded animal. A strong, warm wind blew.

'Let's run,' Amai said. I had always thought of my mother as old. But looking back from the point of view of a woman in her sixties, I realise that at forty-two she was young and active, barefoot, with strong country legs. When we arrived, the clouds were heavy, eyeballing the land with dark angry looks. The wind blew hard as if to warn us of impending danger, but the rain had still not started to fall. At the homestead I noticed the same arrangement as in Bumburwi, where we had lived. There were two rondavels for living in and a storeroom. The land around the homestead had been cleared and a wire fence erected around it. Several mango trees, still young, had been planted on one side of the yard. Our mother's fields were no longer some distance from the house but were now an extension of the yard, just beyond the fence. The land was smaller, strewn with rocks and hard, even during the rainy season. There was no river, no meadow shimmering with wild cosmos and no friends.

In the field were a young man and two children, a boy of about seven and a girl who could have been five or six years old. They were gathering together their hoes and other equipment before the rain fell. When they saw us arrive, the two children ran to the house, scattering their hoes and other farming tools, while the young man sauntered along behind them. The boy hurled himself into my arms, followed closely by the girl. These were my sister Margie's children, Tanda and Sinikiwe.

The young man, who was about eighteen years old, held out his hand to me and smiled. I was surprised by how much he looked like Stan. He was tall and slim but well-built with close-cropped hair, a high forehead, small eyes like Stan's and an audacious grin.

'Hello, Maudie,' he said with a big smile. 'I see you are confused – you don't know me, right?'

I looked at him, trying to remember if I had seen him before. Amai walked up to us and said, 'This is your other brother, Patrick.'

'Other brother?' I said, puzzled, wondering if this meant that he was my cousin, for which there is no Shona word.

'Yes,' my mother said. 'You don't know him because he was taken by his grandmother, his father's mother, when we went to live in Makwiro before you were born. He came sometimes to stay with us when we moved to Bumburwi, but you were always at school. He comes after Margie and Abigail was born after him.'

I was not sure what to make of this revelation. How many more of my mother's unknown children were there? First there was Morsia and now Patrick. Were there others? I did not ask for fear of being rude.

'So, Maudie,' Patrick said, 'have you come to help us to work in the fields?'

'No,' I replied with a daring, cheeky smile. 'I've come to eat the mealies and the nuts.' A loud jolly laugh burst, like a friendly waterfall, out of Patrick as he tilted his head upwards to the dark, grumpy clouds.

'Well,' he said. 'I think it is time for us to get to know each other. And you can eat all the mealies and nuts and *magaka* and *nyimo* and anything else you like.'

We stepped into the dark kitchen, heeding the warning that rumbled above us, and then the copious clouds opened and exploded on the earth.

Stan and I were just as close as we had ever been, but he had changed too. He was sixteen years old and spent a lot of his free time with his friends. I saw more of Patrick, who stayed at the homestead more often than Stan. After working in the fields, he usually sat near the washstand under a tree and whittled sticks or mended things or simply looked contemplative while he sipped a fermented millet drink called *maheu*. Sometimes I went to sit with him and told him about school, but most of the time I played with Tanda and Sinikiwe. On Sunday they took me as far into the bush as they were allowed to go in search of fruit, of which there was not that much – certainly not as much as in Bumburwi. This was one of the more wretched, unproductive parts of the land that black people were allowed to keep. Some of the younger village children of Sinikiwe's age shouted, 'Murungu dhunu,' but they were driven off by Sinikiwe, her long skinny legs and bare feet clearing rocks and low-lying shrubs like a duiker.

Patrick liked to tease but not in the manner of some of the women in the village who, as *varoora*, or daughters-in-law, were traditionally allowed to mock in a way that could cut you to the quick. I avoided them whenever I could because they were more than likely, like the children in the village, to call me albino or refer to me as 'white child' and ask me for money. Although it was playful and part of the custom, I did not like it.

Patrick had a gentle sense of humour which I could engage with and throw back at him. He showed me how to handle a plough pulled by an ox and went with me to the village on the other side of the hill to buy one of my favourite vegetables, tsenza. But there was a dark side to him, and one day I was given a small insight into it. It was early evening and my mother had asked me to go and get some wood from the woodpile at the back of the kitchen, as she was about to begin cooking the evening meal. As I rounded the kitchen, I saw Stan kneeling on the ground with his head between Patrick's legs like an ox tethered cruelly to the yoke of a plough. He was drooling and his eyes were bulging. He was trying to push Patrick's legs apart, but not succeeding. Patrick had his back to me and seemed unconcerned about the state of his younger brother. I ran towards him and started to punch him on the back screaming 'stop it, stop it' and started to cry. He immediately released Stan and said, 'It's only a game, Maudie.' Stan had collapsed in a heap on the ground, coughing and struggling to breathe. I knew this had not been a game, or at any rate it had been a very one-sided game. I became wary of Patrick. The next day he left the village. I assumed at the time that he had been told to leave by Amai, who had come out of the house when she heard me screaming. A row had ensued, and Patrick had walked away from the homestead towards the main road. But early the next day, as I emerged from the bedroom, there was Patrick. His hand outstretched, he said, 'Goodbye, Maudie. I am going to Salisbury now. You must work hard at school, OK? I will see you next time.' With mixed feelings of relief and sadness I watched him walk away, and saw him only twice more in his lifetime – once when I was about fifteen years old and was back in the village during a school holiday, and the last time at my wedding in 1973. In 1978 he was murdered by his two brothers-in-law. It was during the height of the black liberation struggle and so the culprits reported him as a terrorist and were not charged for what they did. It upset me deeply, despite our brief association, that he had died in such a ghastly manner and that, because I was living in England by then, I was not able to go to the funeral.

After Patrick left the village, I spent more time talking with Stan. It struck me again, as it had done when I was eleven years old, how articulate and clever he was. His ambitions had changed, largely because of poverty. 'Maybe one day I can buy a bus,' he said when I reminded him of his past hopes, 'but it will take some time because I have to have a lot of money. Right now I can't finish secondary school because Amai has no money to pay the school fees.'

His situation had not changed at all. He had only managed to complete his Form 2, but had had to leave school because there was no money to further his education. This was the sad plight of African children. In the United Kingdom's House of Lords in March 1967, Lord Beswick, the British Parliamentary Under-Secretary of State for Commonwealth Affairs, reported that 'in 1965, out of something like 643,000 Africans of school age in Rhodesia, only 56 were in the upper sixth form; and that whereas the present regime is spending £6.6 million on the white population, it is spending only the same amount for ten times the number of Africans in Rhodesia'.*

Stan told me that he did not want to be a garden boy or work as an office messenger, which were jobs that people who had no education at all would do, and which wouldn't pay him enough. He was not keen to stay in the village and work the land with Amai. No, he was going to join the army. At the time I made no connection between his wanting to join the army and the experience I had had on the bus. Neither did I know about the conditions that had traditionally forced African men, and later women, to find work in the paid economy rather than remain in the subsistence economy. A legislative act of 1894 had imposed a 'hut tax' on Africans, which left them with no choice but to enter the money economy and work for white people in their homes and in various areas of industry. But even after the repeal of the act, the lifestyle and needs of urban Africans in particular had changed. They now depended on money, and young people were encouraged to find work to supplement the family income.

I spent the two weeks in the village helping in the fields, chatting with my brothers and playing with Tanda and Sinikiwe. My memory of that time is of being made to feel special, mainly because I was loved but also because I was different. Amai fussed when I didn't wear a hat when I went outside or worked with the others in the fields. She made sure that I periodically took rests in the shade while the others continued working, even though I was older than Tanda and Sinikiwe.

---

* 'Rhodesia: Education of Africans', *Hansard*, 21 March 1967, https://api.parliament.uk/historic-hansard/lords/1967/mar/21/rhodesia-education-of-africans

I was given lighter jobs to do and no one seemed concerned if I said that I was tired and didn't want to do any more work. I certainly never questioned Amai's decisions, and may, in fact, have experienced a sense of entitlement because I felt different from my family – a feeling that had begun early in my realisation that I was now a Coloured. It is possible that the special treatment I received was the result of a misplaced fear that government officials would somehow find out and, I would be forbidden from visiting the village.

Amai walked miles to procure my favourite fruits or vegetables. Apart from being annoyed when the varoora teased me, I do not remember a single occasion when I was unhappy or longed to go back to school to see my friends. Although I did not miss the convenience of tap water, especially as water was always available, I did miss a flushing toilet.

Time in the village went quickly and, before I knew it, Sisi Margie had come from Salisbury to see the children and to take me back and deliver me to the nuns for my final year of primary school.

Nineteen

My final year at Sacred Heart Home passed almost unobserved by me. I was now among the oldest of the pupils and aside from a craze for Cliff Richard and Elvis Presley, and having a crush over one of the boys, I remember nothing unusual or of significance about that year. There were tests to be written and that remained my main focus.

I had no idea where I would go for my secondary education. My choices were limited to the four schools for Coloureds – Founders High in Bulawayo, Embakwe in the south of the country near Botswana, Morgan High School in Salisbury and St John's High School in Salisbury. I assumed that I would be sent to Embakwe, which was a Catholic mission school and was much nearer to Bushtick than the other Catholic school, St John's High. Towards the end of the year I was told that I would be attending St John's High School. I remember a certain amount of trepidation that, although I would be nearer my family, I would not have any friends at this school. I was wrong about that. There were a few children from Bushtick that went on to do their secondary education at St John's. Jenny, whose mother's surname was similar to mine, was one of them. Despite my shyness and feelings of insecurity, I thus avoided the struggles of settling into my new school. I never saw Pat again, which meant that she had gone either to Embakwe or to Founders High School, the two schools that served the Matabeleland district.

I arrived at St John's High School in January 1963, three months after my thirteenth birthday. I was two weeks late. A relative driving to Salisbury finally delivered me to the school. My mother had been afraid of making the journey from the village to Salisbury because of rumours that police were stopping black people who were travelling from the rural areas into the towns, some of whom, it was rumoured, disappeared into the prisons until their families were told to collect their bodies for burial. I had written a letter to the nuns to let them know that I had no idea when I might come to school because 'there is a war on', a letter that, according to the headteacher, Sister Hyacinth, was a source of amusement to them. I remember writing that letter on Amai's instructions, sitting in the semi-dark kitchen, the rain a gentle whisper through the open gap that served as a window. The 'war' I was referring to could have been the split that occurred between the Zimbabwe African National Union (ZANU), led by Robert Mugabe, and ZAPU, led by Joshua Nkomo, and the public disagreements, sometimes accompanied by violence, that occurred in 1962. Or it could have been the turbulence unleashed by LOMA against Africans, sometimes for the smallest of infringements because African people were now preparing for protracted guerrilla warfare against the white regime. My literal translation of the Shona word for war, *hondo*, projected a conflict occurring on a much bigger scale.

During my first year at St John's I was placed in a boarding house detached from the main part of the school and reserved for the youngest children. I was very skinny when I arrived at the school. Sister Prisca, a Coloured nun, felt sorry for me and decided that every day after dinner I should meet her at the door to the school kitchen and receive a tablespoon of malt extract. The malt regime did not last long, most likely because I decided that I did not like malt enough to endure the daily routine. I obviously did not remain as slight as I had been at the beginning of my early days at St John's, as one photograph in my collection bears witness.

Right near the entrance to the main campus of the school was a grotto with a statue of the Virgin Mary. She was in an elevated position and stood looking down, hands pressed together in prayer. Every year one girl was chosen to carry a crown of flowers to place on the statue to symbolise that Mary was 'Queen of May'. The girl would be dressed in a white bridal dress, complete with a veil, and walk at the back of the procession bearing the crown of flowers, which she would place on the statue's head. The photograph from the year when I was chosen to do the crowning shows a slightly embarrassed face with thick eyeliner running above my eyelids. I was fifteen years old. I barely recognise myself. My face is chubby and framed by a lace veil. The dress I am wearing looks too tight. Either I had filled out by that age, or it had been designed for a very slender bride.

I was placed in Mr Azevedo's form class. I had never been taught by a lay teacher before, let alone a man. He seemed like a giant to me. But I soon learnt that, although a firm disciplinarian, he was gentle and approachable. He taught me English and Latin in that first year and then continued as my English teacher. My favourite subject, however, was French. I felt that I had a flair for the language, but it may be that I did well because I liked the teacher, Sister Gloria.

Science was a different matter. I began quite well and enjoyed the subject, which was taught at first by one of the nuns. Then a male teacher took over. His attitude, however, meant that girls were doomed when it came to science. To him, science was a boys' subject and wasted on us girls. At times when there was a shortage of equipment, the girls would be told to sit in the corner and read while the boys carried out the experiments. I dropped science from my O-level subject choices.

It was in PE and sport that I truly came into my own. I especially enjoyed the gymnastics we were sometimes allowed to do, but I was also good at field sports and flourished as a sprinter, a swimmer and a tennis player, as well as being in the school's 'A' team for netball. In my first year, some girls told the science teacher that I could clear a four-foot-high jump. He laughed and said that it was not possible for a thirteen-year-old girl to do that. The girls insisted, and so one evening he brought out the high-jump equipment – a long rod suspended between two poles – measured the height carefully to four feet and called me to attempt the jump. It had come as a surprise to me too that I could jump that high. I was barely five feet tall myself! I have no recollection of having done it before that day. But far from being nervous or afraid, I cleared the bar confidently, just the slightest brush leaving the bar shaking gently, to cheers from everyone present. Mr Dennis just smiled and nodded his head.

I was a devoted Catholic. I immersed myself with ardour into all the rituals and joined every Catholic organisation available. Unaware of the impression I was giving with my religious fervour, I was summoned one day to Sister Hyacinth's office. It was my final year in the school and we were revising for our O-level examinations.

'What will you do after O levels?' Sister Hyacinth asked.

'I'm not sure, Sister. I will probably become a nurse.'

'Some of the Sisters and I have been thinking that perhaps

you would like to try the novitiate. We could send you to a novitiate in France. What do you think?'

I was not shocked; I was horrified. My mind travelled back to my primary school years, when Sister Frances had made the same suggestion. We were on one of our bush walks one Saturday afternoon and I walked alongside her. 'Sister,' I said. 'How do you become a Sister?' I was not interested in becoming a nun, I was simply curious.

'It's a calling from God,' she replied. 'You have to pray and listen to your heart.'

'Yes, Sister,' I said, not thinking much about it, as my mind was more focused on running around with my friends, climbing trees or fishing.

'Come and see me when we get back and we can talk about it,' suggested Sister Frances.

'Yes, Sister,' I replied, and ran off to have some fun. I soon forgot about the conversation.

The following day, as I played outside before supper, Sister Frances called me. She held a little statuette of St Martin de Porres in her hand.

'Look, I've brought you a statue of St Martin de Porres. He was a Coloured man, you know. You should pray to him and ask him to intercede for you so that God can guide you. If you have the "calling", God will give you a sign.'

'Yes, Sister, thank you Sister,' I said, touched by her kindness and delighted to have been given a gift, which in my world was a precious thing. My memory of it is that it was a little plastic figure, but to me, who rarely received gifts unless they were from charities, it meant a lot.

My lack of interest in becoming a nun might have had to do with a conversation I had had with Sister Apollonis, who said, 'You are a bright child and could do a lot with your life. You must go out into the big world one day and find yourself.' I never forgot that. Becoming a nun would not give me the opportunity to 'find myself', I thought, so I set about praying with all my heart, begging God to NOT call me to become a nun. I would get myself ready as quickly as possible in the morning before breakfast, take my statuette, run to the lemon hedge where we lined up for the dining room and kneel on hard pebbles as penance, begging St Martin de Porres to ask God to spare me from such a fate. If anyone came towards me, I would pretend to be admiring the spiders' webs – delicate gossamer displays shimmering with early-morning dew.

Unsure what it was about me that marked me out so that, even at secondary school, the nuns were keen to marry me off to Jesus, I looked at the wall behind Sister Hyacinth and to the ever-suffering Christ suspended from his crucifix, and felt the cold hand of panic. *What if this constant hounding of my soul is God trying to tell me that I have been chosen?* Sister Hyacinth brought me back to the present.

'You don't have to let me know now, Maud. We'll have this chat again when you have had time to think about it.'

'Yes, Sister, thank you Sister,' I said and fled before I could be handed another statuette of a saint.

Many years later, when I visited St John's with my children, I told them about the nuns' wishes for me. My daughter Marti's response was, 'Well, thank goodness you didn't listen to them, Mother, or we would not be here.'

Two weeks after she asked me if I would be interested in going to France to join the novitiate, Sister Hyacinth called me once again to her office. I thought she wanted to discuss my becoming a nun and was annoyed. I wished she would leave me alone and let me get on with my exam revision.

Sitting with Sister Hyacinth in her office was an elderly white couple.

'These are my parents,' she said. I greeted them and then waited while she talked to them in German. Finally, she turned to me.

'That discussion we had about going to France, Maud. Have you made any decision about that?'

'Yes, Sister. I think I'd like to become a nurse.'

A long conversation took place in German. I stood there fidgeting and wishing I could go and get on with my revision. Then Sister Hyacinth turned to me and said, 'How would you like to do A levels?'

I was surprised and could feel the excitement building up inside me. I had always wanted to go on with school but knew that there was little chance because the 'welfare' system, of which I had been a beneficiary so far, did not extend beyond O levels. Morgan High School was the only government school in Mashonaland where Coloured pupils could do A levels. All attempts by the Coloured community to get another secondary school built to accommodate the rising numbers of children needing secondary-school places had come to nothing. Even if the fees could have been found for me to attend Morgan High School, I would still have been faced with the problem of accommodation, living expenses, pocket money and so on.

'I would really like to do A levels, Sister. But if I went to Morgan I would have nowhere to stay, and my mother couldn't afford it.'

'We are not talking about Morgan,' she said with a smile. 'My parents could pay for you to attend the Dominican Convent and you could stay here at St John's. You could catch a bus every morning from the main road if there is no school car going to the Convent and come back on the bus. What do you think?'

I stared open-mouthed at Sister Hyacinth. The Convent was an expensive white school, which, as a private school, was allowed to take a small proportion of pupils from non-white backgrounds. I was not sure if I had totally understood what she was saying and was unable to respond. I began to wonder what the catch was. Were they sweetening me up for the novitiate? Or perhaps they would want me to work for them as a maid in Germany. But then they could take me after O levels. They did not have to pay for me to do A levels at an expensive white school just to become their maid.

'So, what do you think, Maud?'

I looked at Sister Hyacinth and burst into tears. I was not sure if they were tears of joy, of gratitude, or of amazement that I should be considered worthy and deserving of such a generous offer. In between my sobs I could hear concern in her parents' voices and I felt Sister Hyacinth's arm around my shoulder.

'All right, my dear, pull yourself together. Go back to your studies and we will arrange everything,' she said kindly, and took me to the door.

Twenty

I enjoyed my time at St John's and proved myself both aca-
demically and in sport. I had many friends and do not
remember any enemies. Among my friends was a girl called
Stella who had been orphaned when she was a little girl. She
and her sister sometimes stayed at school during the holidays.
As there were usually only four or five children who stayed at
school, we did everything together and then went back to our
usual friends during term time. I generally went to the village
just once a year. When I reached the age of fifteen, I had other
interests and preferred to spend the long school holidays with
my friends in Bulawayo or with cousins in Shabani (now
called Zvishavane) or Salisbury – particularly Arcadia, one of
the areas designated for Coloured residence. Arcadia was for
me one of the most exciting places, with regular events at the
Community Centre, especially dances and beauty contests,
not to mention the many Coloured boys seen hanging around
by the service station near the Community Centre.

Arcadia is about a mile from town. Walking with my
friends to town was one of the things I enjoyed most about
spending time there. We watched the to-ing and fro-ing of

people along the road, the many cars, and the ice-cream men on their bicycles with their refrigerated carts. The ice cream was to us the best in the world. I enjoyed spending time in Arcadia, yet I never felt that I belonged to that community. I felt the same about my mother's village after she moved from Bumburwi, her maternal family home, to Hakata in the Murehwa district, where her father was the Headman. In Hakata village I had no friends and knew hardly anyone, even though the bulk of the village population were members of my mother's paternal family. I had nothing to do besides help my mother. I felt a true sense of belonging at my mother's homestead, but not in the village as a whole. I made sure to go and visit my mother from time to time during school breaks, but, unless arrangements had been made for someone to collect me from school, I was not allowed to spend holidays with friends or otherwise leave the school.

I recall very little concerning politics at school. Newspapers were not made available to us, we never discussed politics, and even though we studied the United States of America in geography, and it was the height of the civil rights movement, we were not told about slavery, about Rosa Parks or Martin Luther King, or about racism and discrimination anywhere in the world. News of the Vietnam War passed me by until I arrived at university. But neither did we discuss our own local Rhodesian politics. It may be that the nuns were trying to protect us from the outside world, but it is more likely that they were afraid of contravening LOMA, which governed all political action with severity, especially after the ascendance in 1962 of the Rhodesian Front Party and even more sternly after 1964 under Ian Smith. Wrapped up in ignorance, I was perfectly happy, prioritising my studies, my friends and, to a lesser extent, my family. After my mother's devastating information that my father had died,

I had got used to the idea that I no longer had a father and thought little of him, aside from the occasional fantasy. One such fantasy was that the name Lenning was a disguise and that I was actually the granddaughter of the famous Lenin from Russia, and that my father, his son, had fled Russia, but my mother was forbidden from talking about him for political reasons. Vladimir Lenin, it turned out, had not had any children. I did not know that at the time.

I lived in this safe little bubble and did not concern myself with the outside world. Then an event occurred that aroused everyone from all backgrounds in Rhodesia and even got the nuns talking politics. On 11 November 1965 Ian Smith declared independence from Britain. The Unilateral Declaration of Independence (UDI) came after years of failed negotiations over a potential independence deal between the settlers of Rhodesia and Britain, the colonising authority, and it ensured that white people would hold absolute power over Africans in perpetuity. African leaders rejected the idea of independence without the rule of the majority. They had not been consulted over its terms.

I was in the shower when I heard animated talk coming from a group of girls standing outside the showers. 'We are independent,' they were saying, their excitement implying knowledge of the subject matter. I had no idea what they meant but, not wanting to expose my ignorance, I waited until I got into the classroom and then asked my teacher. I remember feeling a sense of doom, and feared war. I had heard enough about African nationalism from Amaiguru Hilda to convince me that this would make African people very angry and could only escalate problems for the whole country. Although white people (and many in the Coloured and Asian communities) revelled in this new political state of affairs, it was an event that added fuel to the engine of African rebellion and hastened the inevitable drive towards the creation of the state of Zimbabwe. The celebration of settler public holidays such as the Rhodes and Founders holiday, a four-day bank holiday to celebrate the arrival in Rhodesia of the white settlers, took on even greater significance for the white population.

I often stayed at school during short bank holidays such as Rhodes and Founders. On one occasion, when I was fifteen years old, I was sitting with my friends Stella and Ruth under the flamboyant trees near the swimming pool. Stella and I were staying at the school but Ruth was going home later that day to stay with Mr and Mrs Jones, her mother's employers. They were a kind white couple who had no children of their own. We were laughing loudly, recalling the time when the Joneses had allowed Ruth to bring a friend and I had gone along with her.

Ruth told Stella the story with some relish.

'Maud was really excited about coming to stay in these posh white people's house. We arrive, hey, and Mrs Jones shows us our room. Then she calls us to the kitchen for some tea and cake. After we've had our tea and washed up, she says, 'Ruth, you know where the bucket and mop are for the floor, and Maud you come with me to the garden.'

Ruth doubled up laughing and rolled on the grass, hooting loudly. Between gasps she continued, 'Poor Maud thinks she is going to be shown around the garden and looks at me with a big smile on her face and walks with her head in the air and her hands stuck out pretending to be a lady.'

She was choking with laughter, so I picked up the tale.

'The next thing I know, I am being handed a large broom and told to sweep the leaves from under the tree. I couldn't believe it. I told Ruth that I'd rather stay at school. At least the nuns don't make us work.'

'To cap it all,' said Ruth, regaining some of her composure, 'at suppertime, we don't eat with the Joneses in the dining room. We are made to eat in the kitchen, and Mrs Jones hands us these huge, rusty-looking knives and forks to eat with.'

We were laughing so much we did not see Sister Regis, our boarding mistress, bearing down on us. I looked up to see her watching us with a slight frown, then she called out my name. I stood up and looked into the kind, elderly nun's face. She smiled.

'Come with me,' she wheezed. She was short, with a jerky walk, like someone who has had hip operations in both hips. She had a slightly chubby, amiable face and happy, twinkly eyes. She wheezed with every breath, as if something heavy was sitting in her throat and constricting her breathing. I walked alongside her to the parlour at the front of the reception building.

'Am I in trouble?' I asked.

'No, why should you be in trouble? There is a nice surprise waiting for you.'

I was even more curious when I saw two people in the parlour – a trim, well-dressed Coloured woman of about forty with a large forehead, very short hair and wearing bright red lipstick, sitting by the window, and a tall white man of about the same age with thick, neatly cut brown hair and warm brown eyes, who was standing next to her. They smiled at me.

Sister Regis introduced them.

'This is Mr and Mrs Selby. They have come to take you out for the long weekend.'

I had no idea who these people were and, perplexed, I looked at Sister Regis for an explanation.

'Oh, you poor thing,' said the woman, standing up and coming to give me a hug. 'You won't remember me because you were a very little girl when I last saw you. How old are you now? Fifteen? Sixteen? You were six or seven years old when I last saw you. I went to collect you from the Convent because your aunt had missed her train or her bus or something and didn't make it to the station to meet you.'

I did not remember her, though I remembered the station incident. I did not say anything. Sister Regis took my arm.

'Come, you need to pack your bag very quickly. We mustn't keep these kind people waiting.'

On the way to the dormitory, I turned to Sister Regis and said, 'But Sister, I don't know these people.'

'Don't worry,' Sister replied, taking my hand and patting it. 'Your mother has given her permission. They often take children out who have nowhere to go. They are good Catholics and have a nice home.'

I remembered the Joneses and started to giggle.

'What is so funny?' Sister Regis asked.

'Nothing, Sister,' I said. 'Can Ruth and Stella help me with my packing?'

'Why do you need two people to help you pack? You only need a small bag.' I stopped and looked at her pleadingly.

'Oh, all right,' she said. 'Now go upstairs and I'll call them.'

I had just begun to put some things into my bag when my two friends appeared.

'Where are you going?' they asked.

I shrugged my shoulders. 'There are people waiting for me in the parlour. Don't know them.'

'Knowing your luck, they'll probably turn you into a slave,' Stella said, and our laughter echoed through the empty rooms and corridors, prompting Sister Regis to come to the door and stand there until I had finished packing.

'Now, remember to be polite and helpful at all times,' she said, ushering us down the stairs. Ruth let out a loud cackle and we were convulsed once again.

'What is the matter with you girls today?' Sister was irritated.

'We were just reminding Maud not to forget to mop the floors and clean the toilets,' said Stella, hardly able to contain herself. Sister Regis looked up, as if pleading for help from above, and went into her office.

My friends walked with me towards the parlour. The visitors were standing outside talking to another nun.

'I've seen that woman before,' Stella said. 'Isabel stayed with her. She didn't like her.'

Suddenly the atmosphere between us became solemn. I did not want to go away with these strangers and Stella's remark bothered me. But I had little choice, and after rapid hugs with my friends, I was being driven out of the school gates.

The Selbys lived in Braeside, an area that was mainly working-class white people but had a section near Arcadia for aspiring Coloured people. The Selbys had no children of their own. Their house was quite small, but to me it was a palace. The sitting room had large, comfortable, cottage-style sofas, a green carpet throughout, lace curtains that had frills all the way round and something that made my heart skip – a television. That evening I sat with the Selbys and for the first time in my life I saw the black-and-white images, like magic, flitting across the screen. Appropriately, my first introduction to television was the American comedy *Bewitched*.

I had my own bedroom, something that I had never had before, and I was excited even though it would be for only three nights. Wherever I had been before I had always shared a room with my friends or with family. The room was painted a light blue and there were dark blue curtains on the windows. The carpet was a mixture of colours, with blue dominating. There were two single beds in the room with quilted white covers, a wardrobe, a chest of drawers and a dressing table. I hung my two dresses in the wardrobe. There were a few clothes in it, a pair of shoes and a long red-velvet dressing gown. I examined them curiously. The dressing table also had a few items – a hairbrush, a comb and a small bottle of perfume. I added my comb, brush, eyebrow pencil, deodorant and a pair of earrings to the collection. Then I sat on the bed and wondered what it would be like if the Selbys adopted me. I liked the thought of having Mr Selby as a father. He seemed gentle and caring, if rather quiet and detached. I would have this room to myself, watch television every day, eat in a proper dining room and have a maid to cook and clean like most of my friends seemed to have. I fantasised about going home every weekend, inviting Stella and her sister and maybe Ruth to stay, going to the seaside in Mozambique during the long holidays and going out with my friends who lived in nearby Arcadia. I imagined meeting a nice Coloured boyfriend with a job, getting married and having a house in Braeside, where our children would have their own bedrooms. Little did I know that at that very time in the mid-sixties there was so little employment for Coloured males that a committee of leading Coloureds had to lobby the government to create opportunities for them. Coloured youth with nothing to do hung around a tree generally known as 'The Evil Tree' in Arcadia, drinking the special Rhodesian beers or smoking marijuana, more commonly known to us as *dagga*.

At supper that evening Mrs Selby asked me questions about my life – what it had been like at primary school, where I went on holiday, how often I saw my mother, if I liked secondary school, what I would do when I had completed my O levels. I answered all her questions happily. At that time I thought that I might become a nurse after my A levels. They were both impressed. Mr Selby nodded his head and said, 'Good profession for a girl,' and continued to eat quietly but listening intently. He did not say much. We talked about many things before going into the sitting room to watch the television.

The following morning I woke up to the sound of Mrs Selby's voice in the garden. I parted the curtains cautiously and peeped through the small gap. There was another woman with her and they were sitting with their backs to the house under what I recall to have been a frangipani tree. Mrs Selby had left some cooked boerewors, a South African sausage, in the kitchen. I ate quickly and then headed for the garden. Mrs Selby did a half turn when she heard me shutting the back door, and beckoned to me.

'Come here, my dear,' she said, then called to the gardener to bring another chair.

'This is Auntie Rash. She's my friend.'

Rash, it turned out, was a nickname, probably from the name Rashida. She was a small, round woman whose feet barely touched the ground as she sat. She had very dark skin and long frizzy hair hanging down her back. I marked her out as a Moslem with her distinctive (in Rhodesia) mixture of African and Arab. She gave me a big smile and I warmed to her instantly.

'Hello, Auntie Rash,' I said, bending down to kiss her.

'We will have to fatten her, Mrs Selby,' she said, taking my hand and squeezing it. 'Nothing here but skin and bone.'

'Well, we don't want her getting as fat and ugly as you, Rash.'

I winced. I was immediately struck by the status difference between the two 'friends'. Auntie Rash never addressed Mrs Selby by her first name, while Mrs Selby only ever called her 'Rash' and liberally sprinkled her remarks with insults and put-downs. Many of the put-downs involved Auntie Rash's skin colour. Auntie Rash smiled and looked at me as if to say 'all water off a duck's back'. Nevertheless, I was affronted and decided that I could never live with Mrs Selby. I remembered Stella's remark about Isabel.

'Can you cook?' Mrs Selby asked me as we got close to lunchtime.

'No,' was my honest reply. 'I've never had a chance to try.'

'We'll have to show her at least one dish before she goes back to school, won't we Mrs Selby?' said Auntie Rash, smiling at me and holding my hand as we went to the kitchen for sandwiches.

'Rash makes the best mango pickle. If you are nice to her maybe she'll give you some to take to school,' Mrs Selby said as she cut thick slices of bread and gave me the butter to spread. I was delighted to hear this. A lot of children brought mango pickle to school – it was the most popular condiment to help spice up the otherwise bland food we were given.

That afternoon Auntie Rash showed me how to make a simple chicken curry before she went home. Encouraged by Mrs Selby, I took a walk to Arcadia to visit my cousins, the Franks, and came back after six o'clock. Mrs Selby was furious with me.

'I wasn't expecting you to be away so long,' she ranted. 'I can't have you wondering around Arcadia with all those bad boys and dagga smokers.'

I was shocked but apologetic. 'I spent the whole time with my cousins at their house. I didn't go anywhere else,' I said.

'If they want to see you so much, why don't they invite you to spend the holidays with them? You are supposed to spend time at my house, not theirs.'

I was confused by this. My cousin Moffat had come the previous evening to ask if he could take me to his home to meet his family. Mrs Selby had refused to let me go. By morning she had clearly changed her mind and had encouraged me to go, but had not specified a limit to my visit. I did not say anything.

It was dinnertime. Mr Selby managed to prise himself away from the television and joined his wife and me at the table. We were having Auntie Rash's chicken curry with rice. Mrs Selby ate quietly, except for the occasional comment to her husband. Then she told Mr Selby that I had cooked the chicken curry and did not mention Auntie Rash.

'Good, good,' Mr Selby remarked and carried on tucking into his meal. Having thus set the scene, Mrs Selby began to ask me questions that would change my life for ever.

'So, Maudie,' she said, 'where did you get the name Lenning?'

I immediately answered, 'From my father.'

'It couldn't have been from your father. Did you ever meet your father?'

'Well, he looked after me when I was little, but my mother said that he died when I was about three years old.'

'But who told you his name was Lenning?'

'My mother.'

'But why would your mother give you the wrong name for your father?'

Mr Selby cut in. 'Leave the girl be, Liz. She's only just arrived.'

I was stunned by what she said. What did she mean 'the wrong name'? She looked at her husband and with obvious irritation said, 'I know her mother. She is Annie's auntie. Maudie's father was not called Lenning. I am just curious to know who Lenning was.'

'But my mother said that my father's name was Lenning. She even showed me a picture of him,' I said.

'Well, your mother lied to you,' she remarked. 'I met your father and his name was not Lenning.' Mr Selby cut in again. 'Don't you think you should discuss this with her mother, Liz? The girl obviously doesn't know what you are talking about.'

I realised that she was enjoying my discomfort and I was grateful to Mr Selby for disapproving of her line of conversation, but a can of worms had been opened and I could not stop.

'So who was my father, then?' I asked.

'Your real father was called Strickland,' was her casual reply.

There were so many questions that I wanted to ask her. But my tongue was frozen, my brain seemed to be stuck in something and I could not free it. It was as if an elephant had picked me up, whirled me around, and sat on me, all at the same time. Everything around me had turned into a dark blur. So Mr Lenning was not my father? Who was he? And if my father was called Strickland, why did my mother not tell me the truth?

Back at school I confided in Stella.

Stella tried to reassure me. 'I think she's the kind of woman who likes to cause trouble. She's probably lying or mistaking you for someone else,' she said.

I was not so sure, but I decided that I would not think about it and tried to file the information in the back of my mind until I had seen my mother.

The opportunity to ask my mother came shortly after I had finished my O levels and I was spending a couple of weeks in the village before going on holiday to Malawi with my friend Margaret, and then to the Dominican Convent to do my A levels.

I was sixteen at the time. Amai and I had gone into the bush to fetch wood. I enjoyed these expeditions with her and always looked forward to the quality time we spent together. Alone with just Amai, the birds, and the call of baboons in the distance, I asked her many questions – about her youth, about my grandparents, about the kinship system which is still such a puzzle to me. Being older and wiser, I was no longer afraid to speak Shona, so communication was easy and comfortable.

I had difficulty broaching the subject of Mr Strickland and decided to talk about Mr Lenning, the man she said was my father, who had died when I was three years old. I hoped that now I was older she would tell me who my biological father really was. She had previously told me that Mr Lenning had saved my life when I was born by rushing her and me, prematurely born, to Kutama Mission Hospital. He was the man who gave me the name Maud and whose second name I also took.

'What was Mr Lenning, a white man, doing in Makwiro?' I asked, playing along and biding my time before asking the question I really wanted to ask.

'He was stationed there, building the main road from Makwiro to Norton. He lived in a caravan not far from my sister's farm, where we were living. I used to go and sell eggs and vegetables to him.'

My mother was not a talkative person and I needed to ask her lots of questions if I wanted to get any information. I decided to ask her about her mother's reaction to the pregnancy.

'What did Ambuya Chiraswa say when you told her you were expecting a baby from Mr Lenning?'

I was giving her a hook from which to hang the truth. This was her chance to say, 'Actually, you were not his child . . .' but she did not bite.

Instead she said, 'When I became pregnant I told no one, not even your grandmother. I tried every known trick to have an abortion. I even went to a n'ganga for help. I wanted to get rid of the pregnancy before anyone found out. Eventually I had to go to your grandma when nothing I did worked. She was angry with me for wanting to have an abortion.' There was a long pause, and I feared she'd had enough of talking.

'So what did you do?' I asked

'At first she told me to offer the baby to Mukoma Hilda, because she had only one child, but Hilda refused to take you because she thought that having a white man's baby might bring her more problems than she was prepared to handle. I will never forget what your grandmother said. She said, "So give me the baby. I'll raise it. This is the child that will one day take care of me in my old age." She loved you from the minute she set eyes on you.'

'She died before I could fulfil her wish,' I said.

'Yes,' Amai continued. 'You were five or six years old when she died. Not long after you went to school.'

'My father died about the same time, didn't he?'

'I don't know what happened to him. He might even be dead now because he was an old man.'

I looked at Amai, puzzled. She had told me quite distinctly when she visited me at my primary boarding school that my father, Mr Lenning, had died when I was three years old. Was she talking about Strickland? I was silent, trying to assimilate what she had just said.

'I know,' she said, responding to my pensive look. 'I told you a long time ago that your father had died. It was just the easiest way to explain things to you at the time. You were just a little child. The truth is that I never saw him again, so I don't know what happened to him.'

In my childhood and early teens, the information that my father had died was all I had needed. Aside from occasional speculation, I had been content with that as an explanation for my father's absence until I was fifteen, when Mrs Selby told me about Mr Strickland. The one person who could release me from this cruel suspense was my mother. Finally, I plucked up the courage to raise the subject that was sitting so heavily on my chest.

'Amai, is my real father called Strickland?'

There was a long pause and then Amai said quietly, in an unfamiliar voice, 'Who told you this?'

'Mrs Selby. She said that his name was Strickland and that you used to work for him in Salisbury. She said that Mrs Bhana arranged for you to work for him.'

She stopped in her tracks and looked at me with a thoughtful and sad expression. Then she adjusted her head-scarf, as if she was playing for time before having to make an important announcement. Finally, in a voice intended to close off all further discussion, she said, 'I last saw your father when you were three years old, and he was called Wilfred Lenning.'

Having collected enough wood, we began to look for herbal plants, and she directed me to dig up a root, pick leaves and cut bits of bark from selected trees, as if the subject of my biological father had never been raised. At one point she paused in her tracks to say, 'Listen to that. It's a *timba* somewhere in those trees.' I searched the trees for the yellow warbler and listened, but my thoughts were going hither and thither and my somersaulting emotions removed all ability to concentrate. Why would she not talk about Mr Strickland? I wanted so much to ask her that question but was afraid of upsetting her. I was still nowhere in my understanding. Did Mrs Selby make the whole story up?

We picked and ate mazhanje, many of which had fallen from the trees and lay spread on the ground like manna, filling the air with its sweet scent. I like mazhanje, apart from the skin, which covers the flesh of the fruit like an old woollen jacket. The four large pips are huddled in the centre like a lotus flower and are covered in soft, sweet flesh. You split the skin and vacuum the pips into your mouth in one 'shlumpy' movement and let your tongue play around with them, stripping them naked until they are like clean white bones. You spit the pips out one after another while the soft, sweet, juicy meatiness slides effortlessly down your throat. Yet I could not taste anything, my brain having secluded itself in misery. It was cool under the trees on that stifling hot day. We both feigned cheerfulness, but it was clear that something had changed. I wanted to scream. Why was I being punished? I wanted to tell Amai to let go of my life. It was no longer her issue alone. It was mine and I wanted some control of it. But I did not dare to raise the subject again.

The warbler, in the meantime, continued its happy song.

Twenty-One

I was the only non-white pupil in the lower sixth form at the Dominican Convent. I was surprised by how friendly the white girls were towards me. Not once was I verbally abused or socially excluded by anyone at school. The only white people I had socialised with so far were Lucy and Jackie, and that was six years earlier, when I was barely twelve years old. I was able to settle into my studies quickly and knuckle down. I had decided to do English, French and history, my strongest O-level subjects.

My English teacher was Mrs McLean. She was a very good teacher and although she ignored me most of the time and made unkind comments in my exercise book, I was entranced by her ability to stretch my imagination in ways I had experienced only once before, with Sister Apollonis at primary school.

My relationship with Mrs McLean was mixed. I was afraid of her, so I was extra-conscientious in order to try and please her. However, despite my confidence and success at St John's, I found that at A level my cultural understanding of British literature was limited. Mrs McLean taunted me with comments like, 'This is not what Hardy meant, but then I wouldn't expect YOU to know that!' A memorable comment was about Conrad's *Heart of Darkness*. Mrs McLean had written in my book, 'Conrad was, after all, talking about savages – no pun intended.' I struggled to understand why she had written that and came to the conclusion that she was implying that I was a savage. She made other comments such as, 'This is just such an ignorant thing to say.' Eventually I began to believe that I would not pass English, and I was so anxious that I spent every opportunity I could get reading my set books and trying to make sense of British culture. I was only too aware that there was knowledge that the other girls took for granted that was new territory for me. I was also aware that they went back to homes with parents who were educated and from whom they got help. I usually arrived back at St John's around three o'clock and would go straight to the library, where I would work until suppertime and then again until bedtime. But with no one to help me, I realised that it was up to me to make sense of some of the subtleties and nuances of the English language. On such occasions I thought about my father. Surrounded by so many white girls at the Convent, I sometimes wondered if I was rubbing shoulders with members of my close family, but realised that I would never know.

My history teacher was a nun. She spoke with a heavy German accent and had a passion for her subject that infected us all. We were learning about Europe between the world wars. I was fascinated and utterly absorbed. As a Catholic nun, she was fiercely anti-Communist and felt strongly against Leon Trotsky. On one occasion she had us write a letter to Oleg Kerensky, whose father Alexander Kerensky had been Minister for War during the Russian Revolution and was, at the time, living in New York.

My French teacher, whom we called Madame, was a

relatively recent immigrant from France. She was my favourite. I had been among the best at French in my O-level class and was also doing well at A level. Madame took a personal interest in me. She praised my French accent and regularly picked me out to read something or answer questions. She gave me French books to read after school and extra homework because, as she said, 'French is the subject you should do at university because you could become a French teacher and go and visit France some day.'

One day Madame asked me to stay behind after the lesson. She informed me that there was a scholarship to a French university being offered and that she would like me to apply for it. It was the end of the term, and the following year I would be in the upper sixth form. Madame gave me a lot of information about France and work to do during the school holidays. She told me that I would have to go to the Alliance Française, where they would speak to me in French and ask me questions about why I would like to study in France. 'You can easily get this. I have a lot of faith in you,' she said.

I was sitting under one of the trees that dot the central square of the school with Mabel, one of the girls who had befriended me. We were waiting for her parents. It was the last day of school and Mabel had invited me to go to her home with her for the afternoon. I could feel the flutter in my stomach and fidgeted and checked and rechecked my uniform to make sure it was presentable. This was the first time that a white girl in the school had invited me to her home. I had been in the homes of people who Sisi Margie and Amaiguru Hilda worked for. They had been modest homes. But Mabel's home was in Mount Pleasant, which was reputed to be a suburb for wealthy white residents. I was curious to see how they lived. Suddenly Mrs McLean was standing in front of us, and she beckoned to me to follow her. Mabel and I looked at each other, puzzled.

Mrs McLean led me to her office and told me to sit down. She spent what seemed like a long time sorting out papers on her desk. I shifted from one foot to the other, crossing and uncrossing my legs and looking towards the door because I knew that Mabel's mother would arrive at any moment. Then she sat down and looked at me. It was a look of concern.

'You have one more year, Maud, to improve on your English. You will not be accepted at the university unless you pass and pass well. I don't think you should be doing three subjects. I suggest you drop one of the other subjects and spend that extra time on English.'

'Madame has encouraged me to enter for a French scholarship, Ma'am. I am hoping to go to university in France, so I will drop history and use that time for English,' I told her innocently.

The muscles on her face contracted, her jaw set firm and I realised that she was already aware of Madame's plans for me. At that moment Mabel knocked on the door and informed me that her mother had arrived and was waiting for me. Mrs McLean said sweetly, 'Mabel, my dear. Do apologise to your parents. I have a lot to discuss with Maud and it will take some time. Perhaps you could invite her during the holidays? I am sure your parents will understand.'

Mabel hesitated, as if to object, but thought better of it and left. I never did visit her home.

Mrs McLean looked at me for what seemed like a long time. My legs felt heavy. Finally, she said, 'I know about Madame's plans for you. I believe she is misguided. How is someone like you to survive alone in France? You can barely survive here, and we speak English. If you don't get that scholarship, and you do badly in your English exam, then you are unlikely to get into the university here, and then what will you do – work in OK Bazaars? Believe me, I say this for your own good. Madame is new to this country and not fully aware of how things are done here. You are far better off dropping French and concentrating on English and history. I believe you are doing well in history.'

I could not see Mrs McLean any more. I heard her voice, but all I could see were my dreams of going abroad crashing to the ground. Apart from Sister Hyacinth's suggestion that I go to a seminary, I had never had an adult sit with me and talk about my future, and I had no one else to turn to. To disagree would be both rude and disrespectful. It did not occur to me that I could study French at the local university if I did not get a scholarship, and Mrs McLean did not suggest it. My throat was a tight knot. Hot tears were beginning to fill my eyes, but I fought them because I knew she would mock me if I cried. I also knew that there was no point in rebelling against her. My life at the school would be too painful to contemplate.

I picked up my bags and headed for the school gate. I realised that I still had all the French materials that Madame had given me, so I went back to the classroom. Tears were flowing freely as I took them all out and placed them in a bag. Then I sat down and wrote a note to Madame.

Dear Madame

Thank you for all your help with my French.
Unfortunately, I won't be able to continue with the subject, as I need to put as much time as possible into improving in English. I will therefore not be applying for the scholarship but hope that one day I will visit France. I am very grateful to you for everything.

Yours sincerely
Maud

I went to the staffroom and asked one of the teachers if they would give the package to Madame. I headed for the bus stop feeling less sure and less confident about my future than I had ever been.

Twenty-Two

I was one of only half a dozen Coloured students at the University College of Rhodesia. I read English and history with a view to becoming a teacher. Teaching and nursing seemed to be the only openings for people like me in those days. When I was at primary school, I had been obsessed with designing houses for my mother in the hope that one day my father would materialise and build one for her. When a careers fair was held for schools in Salisbury during my upper sixth year, I was curious, if not particularly enthusiastic, to find out about architecture, especially as Mabel had told me that her uncle was an architect. The woman on the stall looked at me with surprise and then very sweetly told me that she did not think I had much of a chance of becoming an architect and perhaps the nursing stall would be more useful? I did not bother to stay at the fair but decided to go into town instead.

My years at the University of Rhodesia were years of continuing political upheaval. After the election of the Rhodesian Front in 1962, African political leaders switched from trying to improve life for black people through reform and instead began to organise armed struggle. Under LOMA, the movement of Africans was severely restricted: meetings or gatherings of twelve or more Africans in a public place at any time were banned, and there was an increase in long-term imprisonment and executions. A classmate from St John's High School, Richard Robinson, was hanged when he was found guilty of contravening LOMA. It was under this act that my friend Judy and I, deciding to join a protest march, were rounded up by the police, arrested and detained for two days. We were given prison clothes to wear and got changed with a male police officer standing by. I don't remember exactly what was said, but I do remember feeling scared and insecure. When we were let out, a group of people, some of whom were friends from university, were gathered outside the police detention centre. They immediately surrounded us and wanted to ask questions. Unbeknown to us, this was in contravention of the rule about groups gathering, and we were immediately rearrested and put back into detention.

Something that I did not realise at the time was the extent to which I was ignorant of world affairs. It came as a surprise to me after I had left university that there had been major events in the world that I had not heard of. I have already mentioned the civil rights movement in the USA as one example. This important campaign, which was an inspiration to colonised and exploited black people, especially in Africa during my secondary-school years in the 1960s, passed me by completely. Newspapers in Rhodesia at this time were severely censored. Unless one had access to news reports or news-papers from outside the country, there was little information to be had. The papers were full of propaganda items about the brutality of the 'terrorists' (this was anyone, but especially black Africans, who opposed the Smith regime and engaged in guerrilla warfare against the government) or the successes of the Rhodesian forces against them.

By the time I was at university I had only vaguely heard

of Martin Luther King. However, one story that took up a lot of space in the Rhodesian news agenda during these years was the Biafran War. I can only assume that the Rhodesian government was keen to provide Rhodesians with information about black people killing each other after gaining independence from colonialism, but not about black people campaigning and fighting for their independence from oppression and exploitation.

I enjoyed my years at university. I worked and played hard in equal measure. I had enough money to enjoy myself and go on trips to Malawi, Mozambique and Zambia. An expenses grant existed especially for Coloured students. None of us knew where it came from, but we speculated that a rich white man with a mixed-race child or children was responsible. It seemed unlikely to be from the goodwill of the government! We were not told why, but in my final year the grant was stopped for all the Coloured students except me. My Aunt Hilda told me when she visited England some years later that the man for whom she worked in Salisbury was the very man who administered this fund, and he had promised my aunt that I would continue to receive the money. It was a generous amount, and I was able to eat, buy clothes and go on holiday without a care in the world.

A memorable holiday was a trip to Malawi to visit, once again, my friend Margaret. It was during the first holiday, Easter, of the university year. I decided to take the bus, which was the cheapest way to go. It meant sleeping at the bus stop, as the bus left at 4 a.m. It was a restless night sitting under a tree with people walking about and sometimes laughing loudly throughout the night. But we took off on time and I slept for most of the journey to Tete in Mozambique.

It was a long wait in Tete where the bus refuelled, the driver took a break and people refreshed themselves before continuing on the long drive from Tete to Blantyre in Malawi. I was sitting in a small café having a drink when a white man joined me. After exchanging pleasantries, he asked if I would like a lift to Blantyre. I would arrive so much sooner than the bus, which would arrive well after dark. After some consideration, I accepted. I was young and very naïve.

The weather was hot, the journey was long, but the company was pleasant. The man told stories about his regular business trips to Malawi and some of his adventures around Africa. I laughed a lot and felt perfectly safe. We had met not a single other car or truck on the way. The inevitable moment came when I needed to relieve myself and so he stopped on the side of the road and I went into the bushes and was well hidden from the road. I had just finished tidying my clothes when I turned and saw the man standing a few yards away. He had been watching me all along. He came towards me, took my hand and said, 'Come,' pulling me further into the bush. I realised that I was in the most vulnerable of situations. He could kill me and no one on earth would know where I had gone.

My mind was working furiously as he pulled me along and finally stopped. He began to unbuckle his trousers and I sank to the ground and burst into tears. 'Sir,' I said, 'please don't do this to me. I am only eighteen years old, I have just started university and am the only one in my family who has had an education. They are all depending on me. This will ruin my life completely. Please let's go.'

To my utter surprise, the man murmured, 'Oh shit!' buckled up his trousers and marched furiously ahead of me to the car. We drove in silence until we arrived in Blantyre. It was now nearly seven o'clock in the evening. When we arrived, he stopped the car in front of the Blantyre Hotel and with is head bowed said, 'I am so sorry. I don't know what came over me. I have an eighteen-year-old daughter whose life has been completely changed by having a baby too soon. I don't want to ruin your life. Please allow me to pay for your night in the hotel to make up for what I did.' He paid for my room and left. I remember very little of the actual holiday.

As I had chosen to take up teaching as a career, I had to do a postgraduate course in education (PGCE). One day, during a lecture, I heard someone call another student by the name Jess. As Jess did not immediately respond, the girl called her again, but this time by her full name – Jessica Strickland. My heart jumped a beat and hammered against my chest. I was deaf to the lecturer or anyone else as I stared at this girl whose name was Strickland. Could she be the daughter of the same Mr Strickland that Mrs Selby had told me about? I dismissed this notion. She must surely be my age – we were, after all, in the same postgraduate class. I was sure that Mrs Selby would have mentioned that my father had had a wife when my mother worked for him. Nevertheless, whenever I saw Jess, I scrutinised her discreetly to see if there was any resemblance between us – and saw none. I had no idea if the name Strickland was common or not in Rhodesia at that time. The first time that I had heard the name was when Mrs Selby mentioned my father, and Jess was the first Strickland I had met. I decided that she must be a relative of his but that she was unlikely to be his daughter. My friends were also excited about Jess.

'Go and ask her where she lives, then you can go and spy on him to see if you look like him.'

'Tell her your father's name is Strickland and she will tell him. Who knows, he might want to see you.'

'I saw Jessica. You two look alike. You must be sisters.'

'I saw your twin sister today.'

If you were not white, Rhodesia was not the kind of place where you walked up to a white girl and told her you thought she was related to you, let alone that she might be your sister. Despite the turmoil that meeting Jess had brought to my life, I decided to leave well alone and comfort myself with the thought that the man who had really been a father to me was Mr Lenning, and as far as I knew he was dead.

Although we largely ignored or, more accurately, had come to expect and take for granted the increasing restrictions on freedom and the inequalities of daily life, we knew that there was a line, and that crossing it could lead to a lot of trouble. Publicly claiming a white man as your father would have been on that line. A number of daily erosions of our dignity added to my reluctance to talk to Jess. One was when my basketball team-mates all went out to celebrate the end of the season. I, the only person of colour in the team, was left out. They were either not taking any chances or, more likely, it would have been quite normal for them to exclude me and had probably been excluding me all along. Knowing this and expecting it did not eradicate the hurt.

Other examples occurred during my second year at university, when my white Canadian friend Elaine and I were housemates. We went to a café one lunchtime to sample their beefburgers. The burgers at this establishment were said to be second to none. I was reluctant to go, but Elaine insisted that we should break with convention whenever possible.

'We need to challenge the system,' she argued. 'If they don't allow us in, it gives me the opportunity to challenge them and tell them what I think of their rubbish systems.'

They allowed us in, and the beefburgers certainly were exceptional, at least in my case. To show their displeasure at my presence, they had put a thick layer of salt on my burger, making it totally inedible. It was all done with smiles and feigned good service. Elaine's was fine, of course. She was incensed and would have protested had I not stopped her and suggested we leave. She complained to the waiter, a black man who looked remorseful but could not do anything. We left the café without paying. Had I gone there with another person of colour, they would not have let us beyond the door, but it is more likely that we would not have bothered going there at all. They were not going to turn a white person away, so they found a way of sending me a strong message.

On another occasion, Elaine and I went to a hairdressing salon because we were going to a party that evening and Elaine needed a haircut. I knew that the salon was for white people only, but while Elaine had her hair done, one girl offered to do mine. Before I knew it, I had been ushered into a back room and out of sight of white customers. Well, that was Rhodesia for you, I thought. I was not going to change it overnight by one act of walking out, and even if I had left, they would not have cared. I thought I would take advantage of the offer to have my hair done, especially as the girl talked so sweetly. They finished the awful job they did by spraying my hair with what they said was hairspray but which turned out to be gold spray. I was not offered a mirror. Elaine, who had been unaware that I was having my hair done at all, was surprised to see me coming out of a back room looking like I was preparing for a part in a pantomime. There was nothing I could do about it except go home, wash it out and start again. Many interactions with white people were scarred by petty, unnecessary and cruel acts of spite, so one needed to have a very good sense of humour to be a person of colour in Rhodesia. And such degrading acts were practised more frequently against black Africans than against Coloureds. There were many exceptions, of course, but interacting with white people was best avoided. Examples like these were to me a warning about the power of the system.

Twenty-Three

During my second year at university, I met Rodney, a white lawyer. I had volunteered to join an organisation for which he was the chair, and which raised funds for destitute elderly African people in the then township of Harare (a township created for black people in the days of Rhodesia), now called Mbare, a suburb of Salisbury. Many of these old people had given their whole lives to caring for white families, but when they became too old to be of service, they were sent away, sometimes with a small gift or a little money, depending on the generosity of the employer, but more often than not with nothing to show for their hard work. The assumption in some cases was that these old people would return to their villages and be taken care of by their families. In numerous examples, the extended family had long dispersed, and in any case the children of these elderly people themselves struggled financially with low pay and hectic lives, trying to make ends meet. Some of these old people had moved to the city for work at a young age and had lost both the desire to live in the country and the strength to survive on their own. There were several such retirees – enough to raise the concern of their fellow

Africans, who wanted to do something about it. Rodney, although he was a white man, was a part of their group.

I was drawn to this man, who wanted to defy segregation not because he was a missionary or someone motivated by religion, but simply because he thought it was the right thing to do. He was good-looking, courageous and determined to spurn the white Rhodesian way of life. When I met him, his parents were living in England and he had recently returned to Rhodesia, the country of his childhood. He worked as a solicitor in a firm where he was warned against having a relationship with me. In March 1973, after I had completed my degree, we got married and Rodney was dismissed from his job. The wedding was officiated by Father Rogers, a Jesuit priest who had allowed us to rent a house belonging to the Jesuits in Westwood, the only officially racially mixed area in Salisbury.

As soon as we were married, we started to make plans to emigrate. We were anxious to leave Rhodesia and live somewhere where we could be free of harassment. We wanted to raise our son in an environment that would be devoid of fear and offer him maximum opportunities. I wanted to go to Canada. Not only was the country said to be tolerant and welcoming of people from all over the world, but my friend Elaine lived there. But Rodney wanted to go back to England where his parents lived.

I was filled with misgivings about this idea. Our experience with Rodney's parents had not filled me with confidence that life in England would be much different from life in Rhodesia. They had visited on a number of occasions and always tried to persuade their son to change his 'foolish' ways. When all the bribes they offered him had failed, his father thought that I might be won over with offers that a simple, poor, Coloured girl like me could hardly refuse.

'As you know, Maud, Rodney's mother and I are not happy about your proposed marriage. I would like to offer you something that would be of great benefit to you and your son.'

I was not angry, but instead listened with interest and a considerable deal of curiosity.

'There is a country which is not far from America, where you and your son could have a very good life. It's a country called Jamaica – have you heard of Jamaica?'

I shook my head.

'It is entirely ruled by Coloured people and will be a good place for you and your son. I am prepared to help you settle in Jamaica if you agree not to marry Rodney. The climate there is hot – did Rodney tell you how terrible the English weather is?'

I shook my head again.

'You would hate it,' he said. 'In Jamaica, I will not only buy you a house, but I will give you an allowance to live on so that you need not worry about work until your son is ready for school. We would keep in touch and you could tell me if there was anything you needed. Now, you must agree that is a more than generous offer. I am sure that a girl as pretty as you would have no difficulty finding someone who will want to marry you.'

'I'd like to discuss it with Rod,' I said naïvely.

'I don't think that would be a good idea. Let's just keep it between us. You break off the engagement, I buy you a ticket to Jamaica and pay for you to stay in a hotel until you find the house you want. Then we take it from there. We will see you again tomorrow and you can tell me what you think. But don't talk to Rodney about it. You want to make up your own mind about this. If you really think about it, you will see what a good offer this is.'

That evening I asked Rodney about Jamaica. When I told

him what his father had said, his fury was unbounded. We would get married immediately, he decided, and then emigrate to England. He was sure that his parents were behaving like the typical white South Africans they were, but in England they would be different people and would welcome me once they had got to know me. As it turned out, I was right to have had serious doubts about this. But as it was, I taught at Morgan High School in Arcadia while Rod stayed at home to write and make the necessary preparations for our departure to England.

We decided to travel to England by passenger liner in December 1973 and booked our passage on the last of the Union Liner passenger ships. This meant that we had to go initially by train to Cape Town in apartheid South Africa. Apartheid laws did not allow for a white man to travel in compartments meant for people of colour and criminalised the marriage of a white person to a person of another 'race'. Rodney had to apply to the South African government in order to be allowed to travel with his wife and son. He had to fill out several forms, which he sent to South Africa. Further meetings and the intervention of the British Consul in South Africa finally led to a compromise. Rodney had to sign a form giving up his belonging to the white 'race' and agreeing to be recategorised as a Coloured! This he did willingly, heaping scorn on the ludicrous laws. Our journey to England began.

When the train finally arrived in Cape Town, Rodney, with his new Coloured identity, prepared to exit with me and our son Michael via the *'nee Blankes'* or 'non-whites' exit. An African man approached him and was directing him to the *'Blankes'* exit when a white police officer arrived.

'Are you Mr Blair?' he asked.

'I am', said Rod.

'Can I see your papers, please?'

Rodney handed over his British passport and the new identity papers.

'Where is your family?' asked the police officer.

I came forward with our three-year-old son, Michael, conscious of people staring at us as if we were escaped convicts.

The officer directed the porter to take our luggage and then told us to follow him. He headed, ironically, for the *'Blankes'* or 'whites only' exit and stood back while we went through the barrier. Waiting for us on the other side of the exit barrier were two more police officers, who led us, with our luggage, to a waiting taxi. Rodney was told to sit in the front – we were still in South Africa, and whatever it might say on paper, he was visibly a white man and I was a Coloured woman. The taxi took us to the port where the majestic Union Liner was waiting.

The police officer who had followed the taxi took us on board.

'I have to warn you, Mr Blair,' he said, 'as long as you are on the ship you are on British territory and you can do whatever you like. But the minute you step on land, you are in South Africa. If you are seen with your wife on land, we will arrest you and your wife. I suggest you remain on the ship until it sails tomorrow. Have a good day.'

We settled into our cabin and had our breakfast sandwiches.

'You know, Cape Town is such a beautiful town,' Rodney said. 'It would be a real pity if we had to leave without your seeing some of it. We have a whole day and night. After breakfast, we'll go and have a look around.'

'But what about the policeman's warning?' I said, afraid at the prospect of missing the boat and spending several years in a South African jail.

'We'll be careful,' he said. 'When we see a policeman, we

separate and pretend we don't know each other, or you pretend to be a local Cape Coloured and I am simply asking you for directions.' He laughed a white man's confident laugh, while I tensed with apprehension.

When we left the boat, I carried our son Michael and decided at the outset that I would pretend I did not know this man. I had heard horror stories about the brutality of the South African police and was terrified. I would gladly have remained on the boat. However, my radical husband was having none of it and refused to let the system deprive us of one last glimpse of Africa. I decided to walk slowly behind him, pretending to be just another Cape Coloured going about my own business, but Rod took Michael from me and proceeded to point out the Dutch gables so characteristic of Cape Town. In my state of nervous anxiety, I was unable to appreciate the merits of this beautiful city.

The morning passed unhindered until Michael needed to go to the toilet. We asked a passing man where the nearest *nee Blankes* toilet was. It was a long way away and there was little doubt that Michael would not make it. On the other hand, the *Blankes* toilet was just around the corner. Rodney decided to take Michael to the Gents, and when he came out, suggested that I go into the Ladies and he would wait outside for me. It felt like going into a room full of snakes. I tiptoed in and ran into one of the cubicles. No one had come in, so I emerged with relief, but just as I was about to wash my hands, a white woman entered. She stopped and looked at me and I began to vigorously wash the hand basin with bare hands.

'You need a cloth,' she chided in a gruff voice, and went into the cubicle. I ran out of the building and into the next street before the woman could come out, with Rodney and Michael following hotfoot.

I had only one interval of complete peace and relaxation

during that day's sojourn in Cape Town. That was when we were at the top of Table Mountain. Most of the people who had gone up with us were tourists – they were too engrossed in the spectacular views of the sea and the pretty city below to care about violators of the apartheid laws. We felt we were a family like any other, doing what other families do together.

Getting to the top of Table Mountain had been another matter, however. We stood with a group of people waiting for the cable car. The seats were for whites only and were occupied, except for one. I was physically and emotionally exhausted and wanted to go back to the ship, but Rodney, certain that we would not get another chance to visit South Africa, felt that I would regret not seeing Table Mountain while I had the chance. He suggested that I sit down, and guided me to the seat. He put Michael on my lap and stood behind me with his hand on my shoulder. No white person present seemed to care that I was sitting on a 'whites only' seat or that we were breaking the apartheid laws. But when a group of black workers went by and they pointed and shouted something to me in Afrikaans, I felt certain that they would report me to the police and I would be spending the night in jail. I shivered, despite the warm breeze, at the mere thought of it.

I felt less anxious after we had visited the mountain. I was also relieved that we were at last going back to British territory to eat, sleep and begin our journey across the seas. When the ship glided out from the harbour the following morning, we stood on the deck and I finally took in the little of Cape Town that I could without fear and with a sense of a new and exciting life ahead.

Twenty-Four

We arrived in Southampton on 1 January 1974. The sky was a dull grey, as if it were sulking. *He lied to me*, I thought as I watched Rod's father pile our motley belongings into his car. It did not feel as cold as he had promised, and it wasn't snowing. But there were other more interesting things that were happening to make me feel that I was on an adventure. Edward Heath was the prime minister, the miners were on strike and London was in darkness. I found it all very exciting but somewhat puzzling. I knew nothing about trade unions, I had never experienced a strike and for the wonderland called London to have no lights at night was intriguing, if a little disappointing.

We spent a few months moving from one place to another, house and job hunting, and finally bought an Elizabethan thatched cottage near the pretty village of Finchingfield in Essex. The welcome we received from the inhabitants of our little hamlet was a big surprise. People greeted us with warmth and generosity. One man offered to help with our acre of garden. Another neighbour brought us fresh eggs. The people next door cooked us a meal on our first day. *White people in*

England are so different from white people in Africa, I thought. I needed to let Amaiguru Hilda know. My letter to my aunt glowed with praise for life in England. I was filled with optimism. Michael was happy at school and seemed to have made a lot of friends until one day he came home with a complaint that he was being called a golliwog by one of the boys. I had no idea how to deal with it or how to support my six-year-old son. But I had come from a world where insulting racist labels were commonplace. Children were like that, I thought naïvely, and it was something we would have to live with. In the meantime, we toured the Essex countryside, visited London and had two more children, our daughters Mationesa and Joanna.

In 1981, two events occurred that threw my head into a spin. In January of that year, a fire in a house in New Cross in London killed thirteen young black people who were celebrating a birthday party. The black community in London reported to the police that white men had been seen throwing a Molotov cocktail into the building. This eyewitness account was dismissed and no one was made accountable. This was the beginning of outbreaks of protests, sometimes violent, by black people in London and other parts of the country, as well as violent clashes between the police and black communities, especially black men. My neighbours made disapproving sounds and applauded me for being different from 'these people', whom they called Jamaicans. By 1981 I was fully aware that all black people were called Jamaicans – at least in the rural areas where I lived. An amusing example of this happened on a bus to the town of Braintree where I did my weekly shopping. A woman who sat next to me asked where I was from. I replied that I came from Rhodesia. 'Oh,' she said, looking puzzled. 'And what part of Jamaica is that?'

Then in April 1981 the Brixton riots occurred. I had

come from Rhodesia. I knew that this kind of rage was not simply a characteristic of one nationality or heritage. There was something more profound, something that went beyond simple name-calling. No doubt if my very gentle, softly spoken mother had lived in England, she too would have been lumped together with these so-called 'hot-headed and criminal Jamaicans'.

These disturbances were a wake-up call for me. In that same April of 1981, we moved to Cambridge and I immediately joined the Race Equality Council. I needed to understand the politics of race in Britain and also to contribute towards the fight against inequality and injustice. This led to my enrolment at the University of Warwick, where I obtained a Master's in Race and Ethnic Studies followed later by a PhD in the Sociology of Education, with particular reference to racial inequality. The rest of my career was in education, firstly as an adviser for Cambridgeshire local education authority, then as a lecturer in education for the Open University, with a short spell as a consultant for the Department of Education, University of Cambridge. I then worked as a civil servant, advising the Department of Education on issues of educational inequality, and finally as a consultant and adviser for a London local authority.

Events in Rhodesia had escalated in the years since we'd left the country, leading to the Lancaster House talks in London between Rhodesian prime minister Ian Smith, the black leaders Dr Abel Muzorewa, Robert Mugabe and Joshua Nkomo, and the British government, represented by Lord Carrington. These talks led to the creation of the new country called Zimbabwe in 1980.

We visited Zimbabwe as a family just after independence in 1981 and again in 1983, when our youngest child was five years old and my mother was seriously ill. She was living with my sister Margie in Marondera. There had been a mass exodus of white people from the country after the black government took over in 1980, and doctors were difficult to find. Eventually I was told about a doctor from Czechoslovakia who was himself preparing to leave but who in the meantime was still seeing patients. His cursory check of Amai was inconclusive.

During our first visit I had wanted to ask Amai again about my biological father, but I was afraid I would be met with the same silent anger as when I had last broached the subject at age sixteen. Now I sat with her, frail and vulnerable in a borrowed Zephyr Zodiac car, parked under a tree, while we waited for my cousin and childhood friend Poona to meet us. Mr Strickland was very much in my thoughts, but once again I was afraid to raise the subject. But Amai was ill and looked weak and old. What if she died before I had the chance to learn who I truly was? Approaching the subject tentatively, I asked her if she could tell me something about Mr Strickland. She turned to look at me, her forehead like a series of waves in shallow water, with pain giving her a permanent frown. She looked resigned.

'What do you want to know?' she rasped.

'Was he English?'

'I'm not sure.'

'Was he Irish?'

'Maybe, I seem to remember something about that. But to me it was all the same. White people came from another part of the world that I would never see. I would not have bothered to ask him those kinds of questions.'

She began to cough – short scraping sounds that made her pull a face as if she had tasted something bitter. I paused for a while until I felt that she had settled. She looked up at me and I realised with a leap of excitement that she was encouraging me to ask her more questions.

'When did you go and work for him?'

'He lived in Borrowdale and I worked for him from the end of 1947 until I left in 1950.'

'What kind of work did he do?'

'He worked for the government. I'm not sure exactly what he did.'

She needed to take a long pause and I waited for a suitable moment to continue. When her face looked less strained, I asked my next question.

'What was his first name?'

'Wilfred, but all his friends called him . . .' My mother searched her memory. 'I think they called him Will.'

I realised right away that she had started talking about Wilfred Lenning, whether deliberately or because she had become confused, I am not sure. The only information about Mr Strickland that I knew I could rely on was what she had told me – that she had worked for him in the suburb of Borrowdale in Salisbury between 1947 and 1950. I tried to make sense of Amai's attitude. Could Mr Strickland have been violent towards her? Was I the product of rape? Perhaps it was Mr Strickland who had arranged for me to be sent to boarding school and made sure that Amai rarely saw me. But why would he do that? He had never made himself known to me. It did not make sense. Whatever was on her mind, my mother was so angry about it that as far as she was concerned, Mr Strickland had never existed. I wasn't sure if she was also angry with me because she saw my search for him as a betrayal. She looked tired; her breathing was slow and laboured. I decided to leave the subject for the time being and come back to it at some time before the end of our holiday. But the opportunity never arose. I went back to England and six months later Amai died, her secret tucked away in the chest that no longer hurt. She was buried on a little hillock that she had chosen in her father's village of Hakata, and I was not there to bear witness.

Amai died on Christmas Eve 1983, aged sixty-three. I discovered an interesting coincidence during a search for Mr Lenning: that he had died in 1963 aged eighty-three! I missed my mother's funeral. In my state of shock, I had picked up the wrong passport and had to spend the night and Christmas Day at Heathrow Airport until my husband delivered the correct one. My memory of Heathrow at that time is vague. What I do remember is the feeling of incredulity as the gentleman at the security barrier looked at my passport and said, 'You won't be able to travel with this passport, miss.'

'Why not?' I asked, peering at the page he was showing me.

'It's out of date. This passport is no longer valid,' he replied.

I looked more closely and realised that I had indeed picked up an expired passport.

'But my mother has died,' I pleaded. 'I have to go, otherwise I'll miss her funeral.'

'I am very sorry for your loss, miss. But unfortunately, I can't let you go through. You must have a valid passport. Do you have a valid passport? Can anyone bring it for you? You could see if there is another flight that will get you there on time.'

My flight was leaving at nine o'clock that evening. In my memory, the airport seemed empty. I was walking away from the security barrier, stunned and unsure what to do when I felt a hand on my elbow. The same security officer was standing next to me.

'Come, let's see what we can do to help you,' he said, and led me to the information desk.

There was a British Airways flight the next evening. There was not much point in my husband driving through the night with the children, so the security officer suggested that I ring and ask him to bring the passport in the morning.

That meant Christmas Day. I remember this kind man taking me to a telephone booth and dialling for me after I had dropped the coins on the floor three times. I explained the situation to Rodney. The security officer asked if I wanted to stay in the airport or go to a hotel. I didn't have the presence of mind to consider a hotel, or maybe I thought it would be too difficult to arrange or too expensive, so I opted to stay. He helped me find what he thought was a quiet corner where I might be able to get some sleep and, wishing me luck, he went about his business. In the context of the busy Heathrow Airport of today, it is difficult to imagine that that level of personal service was once possible.

It was, predictably, an uncomfortable night with only intermittent drips of sleep. I sat up most of the night feeling numb and finding it impossible to imagine my mother no longer alive. I thought about the times I had come home from school to visit her. On every occasion she had done a little dance accompanied by ululation to welcome me. On every occasion she had killed a chicken in my honour. She treated me like a precious gift that needed protecting from neighbours, relatives, the sun and hard work. She had been due to visit us and I regretted deeply that she had not been able to go on what would have been, to her, the adventure of a lifetime. That night I did not miss or even think about a father. I missed my Amai.

The funeral took place on Boxing Day and I arrived after the event. Zimbabwe was going through a difficult time, with petrol shortages making it impossible for those in the rural areas to access medical or any other kinds of services. My mother had to be buried within two days, no post-mortem, because of course there was no way of taking her to a mortuary. Her homestead was teeming with people from her village and from other villages around where she was known, mainly because of her knowledge of herbs and traditional medicines and her work as the local midwife. I was unable to cry, which must have shocked the people present. I tried to keep away from people and found a spot under a shady tree where I sat and tried hard to imagine that my Amai was no longer with us. It was only on the next day, when I was ensconced with my friends in Harare, that the floodgates opened.

Twenty-Five

In 1985, two years after Amai died, I went back to Zimbabwe. This time I was there for a full year with my children. My husband visited whenever he was not on one of his business trips to America.

Sisi Margie was out of work, so I invited her to come and live with us. We talked a lot about our family, our lives, my going to boarding school and my two fathers. It had always surprised me, and does still, that I had family who showed no envy or resentment towards me for all the benefits I'd received and of which they were deprived. Margie had met Mr Strickland on two occasions when she visited Amai, but had been only seven or eight years old and had not known about his relationship with our mother. She suggested that we drive to Zvishavane to see our cousin, Mrs Bhana. Mrs Bhana confirmed that Mr Strickland, and not Mr Lenning, was my biological father.

'I wanted to adopt you, you know,' she said, 'but Ambuya Chiraswa refused. I knew your mother was pregnant, because when Strickland chased her away, she came to my house. We were still living in Salisbury at that time. She told me not to tell anyone, because she wanted to have an abortion. Mr Strickland didn't want to have anything to do with her and she was so worried, you know, because she already had all these other children.'

That would have been the perfect time for me to find out everything I needed to know about Mr Strickland. Yet strangely, I made no effort to talk to other people who had known him and were still alive. Mrs Bhana mentioned a couple of men from the Coloured area of Arcadia who had known him. Another of my uncles was said to have been a good friend of his. My life was busy enough with teaching, caring for the children, sightseeing, visiting friends and family and simply negotiating the complications of life in a new and newly independent country. But there was another reason.

One day the children and I were at lunch at a friend's house in Mount Pleasant, Harare. Independence had opened up the former white suburbs to people of all ethnic backgrounds. Suddenly, they could afford the luxurious homes that white people had either abandoned or were keen to sell before they emigrated in their fear of a black backlash. It was another glorious day in Zimbabwe. The cerulean sky stretched like a protective canopy above us as we basked in the perfect warmth of a dry summer's day. Flowers and shrubs bloomed all around us as if in gratitude for the perfect weather. We lazed by the pool and talked about old times.

This old school friend and distant cousin, who is also a Coloured, was doing research on the Coloured people of Southern Africa for his Ph.D. He talked about the responsibility (or lack of it) that white men took for the children they had with African women. He gave an example of a white man called Strickland, whom he had met at a social gathering organised by Air Zimbabwe, where my friend was on the board. This Mr Strickland had seemed overly interested in him.

'These white guys are forever staring into the faces of Coloured people, looking for a resemblance,' my friend said.

I stared at him.

'That was probably my father,' I said.

He laughed, thinking that I was making a joke.

'I'm serious,' I said. 'Although everyone knows me as Lenning, my father was in fact called Strickland.'

This time it was my friend's turn to stare.

'So why didn't you take his name?' he asked.

'Because he was never there, whereas Lenning not only saved my life, but supported my mother right up until we moved from the area where I was born.'

'Did you ever meet Strickland?'

'No. In fact my mother never wanted to talk about him.'

My friend chuckled in his 'I told you so' manner.

'Do you see what I mean?' he said. 'These bladdy white men. They want to sleep with black women but don't have the moral courage to take responsibility for their actions.'

There was a pause in the conversation. I was deep in thought, considering the possibility that I might still meet Mr Strickland, when my friend seemed to read my thoughts.

'Why don't you try to find him?'

'I wouldn't know where to begin,' I said.

'You can always start with the telephone directory,' he said.

I found only one Strickland in the Harare telephone directory in 1985. I hovered over the telephone, my heart pounding, my hands sweating. I was filled with apprehension at the thought that I might say the wrong thing and frighten him away. Would he think I wanted to extract money from him – perhaps through blackmail? What should I say? How should I say it? I picked up the phone and dialled.

'Strickland here,' said the voice at the end of the line.

I thought I detected an Irish accent and my heart raced. My mother had said that Mr Strickland could have been Irish. I told him that I was looking for a Mr Strickland who was associated with the new Air Zimbabwe.

The voice seemed to me to be full of panic. Did I imagine it?

'No, no, that's not me,' it said hastily – too hastily, I thought. 'That's not me at all. I think the Strickland you are after may have gone to South Africa. I'm sorry I can't help you.'

I held on to the phone while the 'dead' sound rang in my ear like an endless echo. Eventually I put the phone down and allowed my emotions free rein. I wept. I was a child again, missing my mother, wanting a father and a nice home, and tired of looking with yearning at the lights behind curtains that hid mummies, daddies and happy children whose only hardship I imagined was to fight over toys with siblings. Mr Strickland's panicky tone of voice convinced me that I had got the right Strickland, but I did not have the courage to go to the address in the telephone book. I determined that it was not worth the effort and once again put Mr Strickland out of my mind. I would be content with Mr Lenning, who had been more of a father to me than Mr Strickland could ever be.

Twenty-Six

It was 1994 and thirty-five years since the last time I had visited Bumburwi, the village where I had been so happy before being taken away to school. I was on holiday with my children and was keen to show them the place of my earliest memories. It was my first visit to Zimbabwe in nine years.

My mother's homestead had been at one end of the village, close to the main road. We parked the car on the side of the grass verge and walked along the dusty road that I remembered so vividly. I began to feel an inexplicable sense of foreboding. There was a 'Wild West' feeling about the place, a haunting silence and what I imagined to be furtive eyes staring at us from hidden places. Houses on the opposite side of the road from where we had lived, which had once been obscured from view, were now exposed like naked bodies – the leafy trees that should have been surrounding them had vanished as if by magic. Some of the houses looked deserted. A complete homestead was slowly falling apart; the inhabitants, together with the birds, had disappeared as silently and suddenly as the trees that once sheltered them. The thatch on what must once have been a storeroom looked like it had been pulled out in a fight. There were big gaping holes in its roof and some thatch hung almost to ground level, giving the house a drunk and bedraggled look. A door in one of the other houses, probably the kitchen, hung obliquely, forlorn and perfectly still, revealing a dark interior that stared out accusingly.

A severe drought had devastated the land. People had been forced to cut down trees for firewood or to leave the land and migrate to the towns in search of work. Those that remained only survived because of the generosity of family members with jobs who were able to support them. Everything looked different. Only the vast canvas of azure sky was still the same.

The first homestead we came to was next to that of my great-uncle, who had been the Headman when I was a little girl. I was just about to shout, '*Tipindeiwo*,' a way of politely alerting people to our presence, when a woman who looked as if she might have been in her sixties emerged from behind the kitchen rondavel. She stopped short, startled to see us. She was barefoot with a skirt that came down to her ankles. Her dark face was surprisingly smooth, as if the ravages of drought and poverty had not yet arrived at her door. Something about her shape and her stance reminded me of my mother.

The old lady, who, it transpired, was my mother's cousin, peered at us uncertainly. I greeted her in Shona and said, 'I am Maud, Serina's daughter who used to live in this village.'

'*Yowe, yowe, yow-ee,* you are Maudie. It's been such a long time. I don't think you remember me. And are these your children? I thought you were living in England. When did you arrive?' She fired these questions at me, all the time holding my hand in both of hers, which felt rough and chapped, and peering into my face. She invited us into the house – the same simple, dark interior that I had known, almost bare, with only a few clay pots and kept spotlessly clean. There was a man who could have been anything between thirty-five and forty-five years old sitting on the bench, well dressed in a dark suit with a beige shirt but holding the jacket and a hat on his lap.

'This is my son,' my aunt said.

He stood up, shook our hands then ushered us to sit on the bench with him. His hands were firm, but unlike his mother's, they were soft, like hands that were unfamiliar with a hoe. I commented on how the village seemed like a ghost town.

'Eeee, life is very hard, my child,' said my aunt. She sat down cross-legged near the hearth and, shaking the large, empty, black-encrusted kettle as evidence, she added, 'We have not had a proper rainfall for at least two years. Everything has died. We cannot plant any crops because there is no rain. There are no cows left – we were forced to eat the only thing that gave us wealth. Some just died – food for the crows and the vultures. Most of the people have gone to find work in Harare and Marondera. We all depend on them to feed us.'

'Ah! Life is hard,' her son continued. 'In fact, people have no choice. They have to go to town, but even there, people are struggling because there are not enough jobs. Haaah, things are bad in Zimbabwe.'

I told them that I was taking my children on a history tour of my childhood and the man, my cousin, instantly offered to walk with us.

Back in the unrelenting heat, a slight breeze blew sand into our faces and twirled with bits of dry grass on the surface of the yard. I used to enjoy the feel of the fine sand seeping through my toes, but on that day we would have been forced to hop about like clowns as the charcoal-hot sand would have nipped at our soft feet. We were just about to walk past an empty patch of land which I didn't recognise, when suddenly my cousin said, 'We are here.' We stared at the place where my mother's cluster of three houses should have been.

'What happened to the houses?' I asked.

'They were all destroyed.'

'Why?'

'Someone who used to live here hanged himself from the muhacha tree.'

I noticed the vacuum created by the absent tree that my brother used to climb.

'How long ago did this happen?'

'Aaah, I'm not sure. But I think it was a long time ago.'

'It's a lovely clear piece of land. Why hasn't anyone built on it?'

'I think they are afraid because they think it is bewitched.'

Joanna, my youngest daughter, looked up at me and asked loudly, 'Did they think Grandma was a witch?'

'Aah, no,' my cousin said, to my intense relief. 'People are only afraid of *Ngozi* – these are troubled spirits.'

'Was he a bad man?' Joanna asked.

'I am not sure,' my cousin replied with a smile. 'Perhaps.'

'Do you know why he killed himself?' I asked.

He shook his head. 'I don't know. In fact, I was not here at the time.'

I looked for the well where the women, including my mother, used to gather. The laughter and chatter – usually at a high decibel – echoed in my memory, but I could not see the well. Then I saw the spindly, almost leafless guava tree, now a ghostly relic of its former abundance. It clung to life, defying nature. This had been our tree, Poona and me. Here we had played in the shade or sat on the lower branches pretending to be riding in an aeroplane while we waited for the adults to go back home with their buckets of water balanced on their heads. The tree did not, at the time, seem to belong to anyone in particular. I was as elated as a child that it had not disappeared, and I walked towards it, marvelling at how small it was.

'What has happened to the well?' I asked my cousin.

'It is just over there.'

He pointed to a hole in the ground which looked at you darkly, as if it might bite your leg off if you came too close. It had been left uncovered. Clearly a sign that no one would dare walk on this patch of land and that children were warned with suitably spine-chilling stories to keep away.

'Have they sunk a borehole somewhere?'

'Ah, no. People go to the other side of the village to get water because they are afraid to come here. So they just abandoned the well.'

'The hanged man?'

'Yes, the hanged man.'

I felt the need to escape, to leave this spot with all its tarnished memories and its cruel pulling at my heartstrings. As we walked along, we saw a road going off to the right with a sign covered with thick dust that was trying to erase the words 'Bumburwi Primary School'. That was where I had wanted to attend school with my brother Stan and the site of one of my earliest memories. I must have been just four years old when, one day, wearing our best dresses, my mother in the shoes she wore only on special occasions and I, running along barefoot, went for what felt to me like a very long walk to the school. We were joined by many other people, all smartly turned out and walking in the same direction. We were attending a school play in which Stan had one of the main parts. The details of the play have dissolved with time, but the impression left was profound. It not only re-inforced my admiration of my brother, but confirmed to me that the most important thing to look forward to in life was school. Little did I realise then what a traumatic event going to school would be for me.

I looked across at the vlei, which at this time of the year should have been teeming with wildlife. The silence was unnatural. There was not a single piece of evidence that there was life of any form in the vacant spaces surrounding the village. The vlei stared back as if to mock us. I had been looking forward to showing my children some of the wild fruits that grew in the area. It was early in the season and we would have expected to see types of fruit like hacha, and clumps of buds dressing the tsambatsi bushes or the mukute trees, but there were none to be seen. All of the trees had gone – chopped down for firewood. A few caricatures of trees, which looked like they had been created out of papier-mâché for a children's play, grew between some graves on an anthill halfway down to the river. They looked as if they were in shock – their lives only saved by their relationship with death. My grandmother was buried there.

The children wanted to visit the grave. We walked back to the empty space that was once my home. I noticed that my cousin skirted the old yard, so I deliberately walked across it, pointing out to the children where the bedroom had stood, the muhacha tree, the kitchen where most of the living took place, and the storeroom. My cousin excused himself and returned to his mother's house, and we walked leisurely towards the small cemetery. I asked the children to sit on my grandmother's grave and took a picture, capturing a moment that I knew would never again present itself. There was a large crack running across the concrete on the grave, as if even the dead had capitulated to the drought. The children indulged me. They never knew their great-grandmother. I do not remember her. But she was all that was left – the last remaining root binding me to that parched piece of land.

As we walked towards the river, I travelled back in time and my children listened, fascinated by a childhood that was so different from theirs. When we arrived at the river, we could only stare. It was a heartbreaking sight. The parched riverbed was so criss-crossed with dry miniature ravines that it looked like someone had assembled a million-piece jigsaw puzzle without joining the pieces together. Here and there large rocks held on tenaciously to the dried-mud floor. The river was so much narrower than I remembered. We climbed down and walked over the jigsaw puzzle until we arrived at a dip in the riverbed. This was where I used to swim with the other girls from the village and where I had nearly drowned. We climbed out and sat down, swinging our legs over the edge. Across the river, the white farmers' sprinklers were quiet. This was the time when the land should have been prepared for planting tobacco. I pointed to a space in the distance, beyond the farm and at the end of an open veldt, to a cluster of white buildings, like an oasis with gum trees reaching out into the sky – a beacon of hope. That was Waddilove, where Amaiguru Hilda had been a boarding matron, where Filida had been to school, and where Stan had lived with an uncle while he attended the school up to Form 2, before leaving for lack of money. I would have liked to go there, to retrace the journeys I made with my mother or with Stan and my friends. But it was too far, and the sun was sinking into the horizon, throwing long shadows over the land. It was time for us to go back to Harare.

I could not leave the country without taking my children to visit Bushtick, so we took the train from Harare to Bulawayo. I was keen for them to experience some of the excitement I had had as a child. It was a diesel, not a steam train, so the experience did not have the same level of romance. Nevertheless, the trip was comfortable and enjoyable. After a brief stop to see cousins in Bulawayo, we borrowed their car and drove the forty kilometres to Bushtick to visit my former primary school. I was anxious to hear news about Sister Apollonis, whom I had not seen or been in touch with since I left the school.

'Ah yes,' Sister Dominic, the Mother Superior said, 'come with me.'

I was excited to be seeing Sister Apollonis again and wondered if she would remember me.

'Is she well?' I asked Sister Dominic.

She stopped and looked at me. She was about to say something then decided against it and we carried on. We went past the office and were going through a small, well-tended cemetery when suddenly Mother Superior stopped. She turned to me and, pointing to a grave two crosses from where we were standing, she said, 'There she is. There is Sister Apollonis.'

'Oh,' I said, speechless. Why had it not occurred to me that she might have died? After all, there were nuns and priests in the outlying regions of the country who had been killed during the struggle for independence. The cross gave her date of death as 16 June 1979. She was seventy. Had she lived she would have been, in 1994, at least eighty-four years old.

'How did she die?' I asked, dreading the answer.

'She was very ill,' Sister said. 'I'll leave you with her.'

I felt a bizarre sense of relief, as if the manner of death would make a difference to her now. I had feared that she might have been the other nun, together with the Bishop of Bulawayo and one of my other favourite nuns, Sister Frances, who had been killed by a masked man when their car was stopped on a trip to one of the mission schools. I felt sad about Sister Frances. She had been so kind to me. I took a photograph of Sister Apollonis' grave and we left.

Among my happiest memories of Bushtick were the walks we took to the river where we fished or wandered around in the bush looking for wild fruits.

'Whenever we were lined up to go on our walk,' I told the children, 'Sister Beatrix, the headteacher, would remind us of her golden rules:

'You never walk alone because you will be thinking bad things.

'You don't walk in twos because you will be tempted to do bad things.

'You do not walk in threes because two will do bad things while the third acts as lookout.

'You do not walk in fours because you are paired off for bad things.

'You should always walk in groups of five or more. That's safe.'

Needless to say, boys and girls were never allowed to go on these walks together.

My children laughed out loud but were clearly also horrified by such antediluvian ideas. Sister Beatrix had had quite a few apocalyptic stories, most of which seemed to be around the issue of sex.

We came to a bend in the river and saw two women digging in the sand. They were digging for water. There was no water for miles around except from private boreholes, such as the one at the school. The people in the surrounding area would probably not have thought of asking at the school, which needed to water so many children. All that the women could get was the water that seeped through the sand if they dug deep enough. The Matabeleland area had been hit worse by the drought than Mashonaland. For two years it had been impossible to plant anything and anyone without the choice to migrate to town depended on relatives who worked or hustled for a living in Bulawayo.

We continued along the dry sandy riverbed. I pointed out the favourite fishing spots and the approximate place where I had fallen into the river, ever competitive and desperate to catch bigger fish than the other children. It all looked very different with the sparse vegetation. Those had been happy times. The nuns would give us twine and little hooks and allow us to dig for worms, and we would sit on the river's edge and fish. We always went back to school with something to cook in little tins that the nuns saved for us, on an open fire outside the dormitory. If we did not want to fish, we ran around in the bushes playing hide and seek, taking special care not to tangle with the vicious thorns from the acacia trees, or if it was the season, we looked for wild fruits, which were plentiful.

We left Bushtick and went back to Harare. It was almost time to go back to England, so I decided to make use of one of the remaining days to visit the archives to see what I could find out about Mr Lenning. That visit started me on another one of the significant twists and turns in my life.

In the archives I found no one and nothing associated with the name Lenning. I did find some not very useful information about a Mr Lanning, and considered the possibility that this was my primary-school friend Jenny's grandfather. The spelling, with an 'a' and not an 'e', had confirmed for Jenny's mother that I was not her half-sister. I was still absorbed in my search when my daughter Joanna tapped my shoulder. I followed her to the microfiche she had been scanning.

My heart did a somersault. On the microfiche was reference to a newspaper article from which, when we found it, stared the face of a Mr J. C. Strickland, senior civil servant, Irish, with two children. While I had been absorbed in searching for Mr Wilfred Lenning, my daughter had been busy ferreting around looking for Mr Strickland – and she had found him. My hand shook as I took a copy of the article and, my brain frozen with anticipation, I hooked my arm into Joanna's and we left the archives.

Before leaving Zimbabwe to go back home to England, I took the children to say goodbye to Sisi Filida, my eldest sister, who was staying with her daughter in Marondera – the place where my brother Stan and I had searched for my father. Sisi Margie, who now lived in England but had travelled with us to Zimbabwe, went with us to say farewell to Sisi Filida. As we sat talking, I took the article out. Covering the name, I showed the picture of Mr Strickland to my two sisters and asked them if they knew who it was. Sisi Filida immediately said, 'That's your father.'

Sisi Margie was unsure as she stared at the picture. 'He doesn't look unlike you,' she said, 'but I wouldn't want to swear to it. All I remember is that he was an old man, and this man doesn't look old.'

'You were only about eight or nine years old when you saw him, so anyone above thirty would have been old,' Sisi Filida said. We laughed and left it at that. I was nevertheless doubly convinced that I had found my man.

Twenty-Seven

I kept that newspaper article about Mr Strickland for many years. I would read it and look at Mr Strickland's picture from time to time and ruminate about what to do. The telephone call from 1985 was still fresh in my mind, though I was not certain if this was the same Mr Strickland I had spoken with. Why did I want to speak to him? Was it mere curiosity? Did I want to know him, or did I only want to know about him? Who was he? What was his story? Would I find out something about myself that I didn't know, and if I did, what would I do with that knowledge? How would Mr Strickland react? He was a white man who had spent most of his life in Rhodesia after all. Was he still living there? Something deep and primal seemed to push me towards him. It was both mysterious and fascinating. I knew I did not look like him. Everyone said that I looked like my mother: the shape of my face, my eyes and lips and the distinctive crease on the bridge of the nose were all hers. And yet, as Sisi Margie had said, I wasn't unlike the man in the picture – or was she simply imagining it?

Despite my curiosity, the newspaper article languished in a drawer for nearly ten years before I finally decided to do something about it. I realised that I had very little firm information about my birth father. Sisi Filida had identified him; he worked for the government, something Amai had said, even though I was unsure at the time which of my fathers she was talking about; he was Irish, which Amai had thought was the case. Not much to go on, but enough to reignite and nourish my desire to find him. In 2004 a friend invited me to go with her on a week's holiday to Dublin, which, according to the newspaper article, was where Mr Strickland came from. I had no plan or real idea how to find out about him other than to visit the Births and Deaths Registry and begin from there. Unfortunately, we had chosen the week of Easter, when all public-records offices were shut! I put the article away again for almost four years, when finally I decided to join a friends and family online search group called Genes Reunited and began to search in a more sensible and organised way. I discovered that someone in Dublin had a John Strickland on their family tree. For various reasons, not least being the experience I had had with the phone call those many years previously, it took several months before I was able to send a message to her via the genealogical site. I gave her the information from the newspaper article and asked if this John might be the same man from her family tree. I received a reply from her husband, who was J. C. Strickland's younger brother.

Hello Maud

Before parting with information about my late brother would you please tell me the nature of your interest and where you are coming from. Your name does not make any connection to me or our family research so I would be very interested to make that connection if it exists.

Alan

'Late brother'. I could feel the pulse hammering in my throat and my eyes blurred as I stared at the words, willing them to change. I would never again have the chance to meet him or speak to him. I was devastated. I replied, telling Alan what little I knew about my mother's relationship with Mr Strickland and the circumstances of my birth. I made it clear that I was not seeking acceptance into the family but that I needed to know who I was and also what medical conditions I and my children should be alert to. I received a long reply from Alan with details of known medical conditions in his family, which I have removed from his reply below.

Hello Maud

I have just got off the floor after reading your last e-mail. What a surprise! You certainly have a right to know about him and I shall divide this letter into parts – a CV of him and a medical report.

J. Strickland was born in Dublin in 1923, the eldest of 5 boys of whom I am the youngest. He was always known within the family as Charlie to distinguish him from our father, another John. After school he joined the RAF and was later posted to India. He was demobbed in 1946 and . . . emigrated to Southern Rhodesia in 1947. Prior to leaving Ireland he got engaged to an Irish girl. He joined the civil service in Salisbury and trained as an accountant working in the transport ministry . . . the autumn of 1949 he returned to Ireland and got married in early October.

After a few more years lodging they bought a house in the suburb of Avondale. His career advanced in the civil service and by the time of independence in 1980 [or thereabouts] he was a senior civil servant. He took early retirement in, I think, 1982 to become an Anglican priest. He then was appointed vicar of a parish in Harare where he stayed until he retired again . . . He loved Africa and turned down all suggestions of moving back to Ireland.

During all this time he and his wife had two children, a boy and a girl, who are now, I reckon, 57 and 54.

Well, I have to say that I had to pick *myself* up from the floor when I learnt that Mr Strickland had become a vicar. My thoughts and emotions tumbled from one extreme to another. How did he reconcile his conscience concerning me and my mother while preaching about 'loving your neighbour', 'suffer the little children to come unto me' and so on? One minute I was full of compassion for a man who must have been a good man at heart but had had to live a lie with a wife he loved, and the next I would be seething with anger. Perhaps his wife knew about his relationship with my mother and had forgiven him. Perhaps he had wanted to find out about me, but she had stood in the way. My days were spent on the internet and I emailed Alan with dozens of questions. But he knew very little about his brother's life in Rhodesia, having visited him only once in his home in the suburb of Kensington. My mother had said Borrowdale – but then people move.

My nights were full of disturbing dreams as I tried to make sense of the information I had received. I sifted through my memory to retrieve whatever I could that Amai had said, but I was caught in a maze of contradictory detail, largely because Amai would not talk and when she did, she never made clear whether she was talking about Mr Strickland or Mr Lenning. Now that Mr Strickland was gone, I was desperate to know him.

One day I experienced an inexplicable rage against him, this man who dared to become a priest despite his sordid secret. The more I imagined him preaching goodness to his congregation, the more I felt physically sick. I had been going through this emotional turmoil when I decided that I would go back to Zimbabwe and spend at least two months making further enquiries. I needed to stand by his graveside and talk to him directly. I needed to visit the house where he had lived and the church where he had been parish priest. I needed to speak to the people who had known him and who could tell me more about his life.

Twenty-Eight

It was 2010. I arrived in Harare on a chilly morning at the end of July – the tail-end of winter. As usual, the feeling of having arrived home, even after thirty-seven years of living in England, was strong. The new airport, with its attractive reproduction of the conical tower of the Zimbabwe Ruins, was thronging with people. Few airlines were now stopping in Zimbabwe as a protest against the rapid downward trend in the country's economy and the appalling deterioration in human rights. Zimbabweans, black and white, had left the country in droves. The arrival of a passenger airline was therefore a time of celebration for Zimbabweans, some of whom had not seen members of their families in many years. My old school friends, with whom I was staying, were waiting for me. It felt good to be back.

The road to the airport was in good condition, deliberately well kept so as to hide the real situation from the outside world, some Zimbabweans would say. The more cynical would tell you that it was because the road to the airport was regularly used by the country's then president, Robert Mugabe. At any rate, when I commented that things looked good, my friends decided to take a detour via the suburb of Waterfalls, to show me the size of the potholes that bedevilled all the towns in Zimbabwe. The potholes were indeed large – as my friend said, 'If you hit a pothole in Harare, you come out in Bulawayo.' But apart from the potholes, external appearances alone in Waterfalls would not have told me that the country was still in the throes of a severe economic crisis. Large swathes of land that had once been empty scrub were now boasting hundreds of beautiful new homes – thanks to the émigrés who were preparing for a future return to Zimbabwe or building homes for their families with their hard-earned money, largely acquired from doing menial jobs abroad. After Waterfalls, we drove through town. It looked a little tired and untidy, but it still felt like 'home'.

The once-pristine roadsides on the way to Mount Pleasant, where my friends live, were littered with paper and other rubbish. At that time Zimbabwe had 75 per cent unemployment and no money to pay people to pick up the litter. The big shock was to see the potholes in Mount Pleasant. This had once been among the best examples of the legendary 'Garden City of Salisbury'. Potholes here were a sign of economic deterioration indeed. Zimbabwe, perhaps more than other countries and especially those with stable economies, had suffered greatly under the global economic collapse of 2008. The Zimbabwean dollar had collapsed completely, people had lost all their pensions and savings, sanctions had been imposed by the USA and Britain, and now the only usable currency was the US dollar. There appeared to be a scramble among politicians and senior bureaucrats to fill their pockets with the little that was available, and the country's economy was going into a further downward spiral.

One of the first things I did when I had settled down in my friends' home was to borrow their car and visit Mr Strickland's former parish church, which is but a five-minute drive away from where they live. Sure enough, there was a security guard there who had worked with him for many years and spoke very highly of him. He said what a good man Mr Strickland had been and how everyone had respected him. He advised that I come back on another day, when his former secretary would be in, as she had worked with him for a long time. After all the good things he said about him, I did not have the heart to tell him that Mr Strickland was my father but said instead that he had been my father's friend. I did not go back to the parish after that.

The following day I went to the home Mr Strickland had shared with his wife and family in the suburb of Kensington. This time I went with my friend Margaret. I wondered if I might have walked past or even bumped into Mr Strickland at some point during those holidays when I had stayed at school. My friends and I had sometimes walked to Kensington Shopping Centre to take a break from the quiet, empty school. The Stricklands had lived in a modest house by the standards of Kensington, but of course it would have been beyond my wildest dreams when I was a child. There was a high wall around it with an electric gate. That would most likely not have been there when they lived there. I rang the bell several times and, after a long wait and just as I was giving up hope, a young black woman opened the gate a fraction. She looked as if she was only partially dressed and had thrown something on in a hurry.

'Excuse me,' I said. 'Did you by any chance know the Stricklands who used to live here?' She looked at me with sleepy eyes, then at Margaret, who was waiting in the car, and shook her head.

'Are you the owner of the house?'

Again, she shook her head.

'Are your employers in?' I asked.

She shook her head, all the time looking at me with a blank expression. Frustrated, we decided that we should visit the grave at the Kensington Parish Church, where Mr Strickland and his wife were buried. It was a small churchyard and, by dividing it in half between us, it did not take long to find them. There were no graves but two small plaques lying side by side, indicating that they had been cremated. I felt empty. I could summon up no emotion at all as I stood there looking at his name. I felt no anger and no relief to be finally saying both hello and goodbye. We stood for just a few minutes and then we left the churchyard.

'How do you feel?' Margaret asked.

'Empty, like he had nothing to do with me,' I said, and meant it.

I had done what I could and would let the matter rest. I could now tell my children that while I was in Dublin in 2004 in search of information about my father, he had died in Harare, and focus on getting the family history from his family and from the internet. Or so I thought.

I was beginning to settle into a holiday free of research, allowing just one or two days to visit the archives for information about Mr Lenning, when my sister Margie rang me from England. I imagined the worst because Sisi Margie would not normally ring me from the UK. I was dreading answering, but of course, whatever it was, I had to speak to her.

'Maud, did you find your father?' she asked. I felt the tension floating off my shoulders.

'Yes,' I said.

'I just remembered something. You need to speak to Sisi Tebi. She used to go and see Amai in Borrowdale. She was already a teenager, so she will remember more than me or Filida.'

I drove down a narrow dirt road – potholed, littered with paper and other detritus – from which rocks jutted hazardously, testing the resilience of my friend's small 1965 Ford Cortina, into Tafara township. Piles of rubbish lay like malevolent ulcers on the sides of the road. Rubbish had not been collected for a year or more. Someone had previously burned one pile of rubbish, but there was an enormous fresh pile. A large rat sniffed and dug around nonchalantly. Tafara had been one of the worst-affected areas during the cholera outbreak of 2008 and it still looked vulnerable.

Sisi Margie had said, 'Sisi Tebi's house is just near the turn-off from the main road, where you enter the township.'

I asked her for the name of the street.

She clearly could not remember, so dismissed me with a 'Haaah, you don't have to go far.'

She spoke in Shona. We had always spoken to each other in Shona from the day she arrived in England twenty-five years previously, something for which I was grateful.

'When you turn off the main road and into the first road that goes between the houses, her house is very nearby – *padhuze dhuze*. Just look out for a tall tree with bougainvillea growing right up to the top. Hers is the only yard with a tree like that. Once you turn that corner, you will be there in less than five minutes.'

The trouble was that she had not said which turn-off from the main road she meant. I discovered that there was more than one. A whole hour later I finally arrived at our cousin Tabitha's (Sisi Tebi) house, which was not padhuze dhuze but required several turns to the left, a few to the right; negotiations with potholes the size of lakes and vicious rocks growing straight out of the road; several stops to ask directions to a tall tree shining like a beacon with bougainvillea, only to be met by blank stares; and finally arriving to find a tree, not much taller than any other, and with a bougainvillea devoid of flowers, looking instead like it was headed downwards, dust unto dust, rather than upwards, via the tree, into the sky. It had been more than ten years since Sisi Margie had last visited Cousin Tebi! But I had arrived.

Sisi Tebi, seventy-eight years old, was my first cousin, the daughter of my mother's eldest sister. She was tall and beautiful. She held herself upright as if she had once been a model, although her dress looked well worn and old. Her headscarf was tied elegantly, giving her a regal look. She stood in front of her little house holding a *mutswairo* that was stunted, as the grass had broken and fallen off from constant use. She had just finished sweeping the yard as I parked the car under the tree, and was still holding the broom. She looked at me without recognition at first, then her dark brown eyes lit up as she exclaimed, 'Is it you? Is it Maudie?'

It had been at least forty years since I had last seen her and I only recognised her because she looked so much like her mother, whom I had seen in 1983 after my mother died. She gave me a warm embrace, which, for someone I hardly knew, surprised me. I had brought her groceries, the customary thing to do in cash-strapped Zimbabwe, and we sat outside in the sun and drank Cokes. She had a lot of questions to ask about me and my family and about Sisi Margie. She looked concerned that I had got divorced, congratulated me on having so many grandchildren when she thought I looked so young, and laughed at some stories about Sisi Margie. She exuded warmth and affection.

Finally, I told her why I had come to see her and about my correspondence with Alan, Mr Strickland's brother. I then showed her the newspaper article that my daughter Joanna had found in the archives and that I had brought back with me from England. She looked thoughtful for a few minutes, then said, 'This man doesn't look familiar to me and he is really too young. I saw your father many times in Borrowdale when I went to visit your mother. He was an old man, old enough to have been your mother's father. He must have died a long time ago.'

I looked at her, wondering if perhaps she too was mixing

Mr Strickland with Mr Lenning who, according to a photograph of him, had been an old man, but also feeling as if I could not deal with these twists and turns in my life. All I had wanted was information about what kind of man my father had been, not the news that he was not, after all, my father! I was still reeling from the shock of hearing what she had said when she asked, 'Did you say he had two children?'

'Yes,' I replied, 'a girl and a boy who are about sixty-three and sixty now.' I tried to recall what else Alan had told me in his letter.

'A boy and a girl?' she sounded puzzled.

'That cannot be him,' she said. 'Mr Strickland had two sons. One was about twenty or a bit more, and the other was about my age at the time – about eighteen or nineteen.'

This was too much for me. A visit that had been meant simply for finding out the facts about my biological father – the one whose face I thought I had found in the newspaper article – was threatening to turn my world upside down yet again. Everything my mother had said had been corroborated by the newspaper article and by my sister Filida's identification of him. I was dumbfounded.

Sisi Tebi took my hand and, squeezing it, she said, 'Let me tell you what I know.' She took a sip of Coke.

'Your mother worked for Mr Strickland in Borrowdale. Mr Strickland and my brother-in-law, Mr Bhana, were friends, and it was my sister, Mrs Bhana who told your mother about the job. Your mother worked for him for only two or three years as far as I remember, then suddenly she left and went back to the farm. That's my mother's farm, where your mother had left the children with Grandmother Chiraswa. When you were born, we all thought that she had got involved with Mr Lenning who lived near the farm. He was also an old man.'

'How did you find out that Mr Strickland was my father?' I asked.

'Very few people in the family knew about that. It was only when Mrs Bhana wanted to adopt you and went to see Mr Lenning that he told her he didn't think he was the father. I had got married by then and left Makwiro, so I only found out all this much later. Mr Lenning was very good to your mother and to you, so everybody believed he was your father.'

'Amai said that Mr Strickland worked for the government. Is that what you remember?'

'That I can't tell you, because I never spoke to him and it is not the kind of question that would have occurred to me to ask.'

'Was he married?'

'No, I really don't think so, because there was never a woman there. The last time I went to visit your mother was in 1949, and there were only the two boys there.'

I looked at the newspaper article again, wondering whether I should throw it away. I realised that my anger had been misplaced and J. C. Strickland was an innocent party – a good man, as the security guard at the parish church had said. He had not cheated on his wife with the maid, he did not have a sordid secret to keep, and my biological father had not been a vicar. I could not throw the paper away but folded it and put it back into my bag. What would I tell Alan, and how would I be able to live down the embarrassment? There was going to be no rest this holiday after all. I would have to go back to the archives and look for the real Mr Strickland. I felt as if my life were a series of tricks. The more closely I looked, the more likely it was that what I looked at would morph into something else, a clever magician's legerdemain. I felt weary, but there was one more thing I had to do, and that was to see my sister, Filida, who had identified J. C. Strickland from the newspaper article as my father those many years ago. I clung to a small hope that Sisi Tebi had got it wrong. I needed to close the book on years of searching and wondering and I wanted to see my sister anyway before I returned to England.

Sisi Filida was at her church's headquarters in the district of Chiweshe. There was no way of contacting her to let her know that I would be going to visit her. I hired a driver, and with his car we set off early the following day. We drove northwards through Borrowdale to the A11. Patches of blue peeped through thick formations of white cloud in the sky. The grass alongside the road looked reddish-brown and patchy. There was no sign of rain, despite the dense clouds.

Philimon the driver talked continuously, like a man in therapy. His face was downcast and occasionally angry as he listed the many faults of the government and the misery that corruption had wrought upon himself and his fellow citizens. I listened patiently, only interrupting to ask the occasional question. He had had a good job as a bank clerk but had been laid off when the economy had taken a downturn. His only alternative had been to try his luck as a private taxi driver.

'Nowadays it is difficult to find clients,' he said miserably. 'There are so many of us who are trying our level best to make a living, but there is too much competition for so few tourists. We can't even send our children to school because there is no money. Aaah, this government has been bad for us. They have destroyed the country. They just don't care about Zimbabwe.'

I knew that I was being drawn into a privileged confidence. This was not the kind of discussion he would indulge in with local Zimbabweans. People had been known to disappear for less. For him I was a stranger just passing through, an opportunity to ease the burden of struggle and the humiliations of poverty.

Eventually we were driving through farmland and Philimon shook his head sadly.

'Do you see what I mean?' he said, more as a statement than a question. 'All those expensive sprinklers just sitting idle and rusting. There are no crops in the fields, and we are buying so much food from South Africa, which most people can't even afford.'

As we drove through the Mazowe (formerly Mazoe) Citrus Estates, once the pride of the country's fruit-export industry, Philimon was silent, as if he were driving through a cemetery and he needed to show respect for the dead. The leaves on the orange trees had lost much of their lush green colour. Some branches hung to the ground, as if someone had twisted and broken the arms of the trees. Oranges from the last season lay scattered and rotting. Hills rose behind the estate, casting it in shadow, dark and brooding.

I broke the silence. 'I can still remember the days when you could stop on any main road out of Harare and buy sacks of oranges from stalls on the side of the road.'

Philimon nodded.

'Do you think it was a mistake to take the farms away from the white farmers?' I asked.

Philimon glanced at me quickly then trained his eyes on the road.

'You know, I think it was the right thing to do.' This time his voice had lost its sadness and traces of anger. He sounded formal, like someone engaged in a controlled and well-chaired debate.

'I think it was time to take the land back because the white farmers had such a good life that they would not have wanted to share with us. Some had so much land which they didn't even use. But the whole thing should have been done in a different way, without violence. Through the courts. A big problem is that the farms should have been given to those black people who knew how to farm already, because they had done it all their lives working for the white farmers. They knew how to run a farm. The government should have given them some money to help them. The problem is the corruption, because it is the politicians who grabbed the farms for themselves, and they know nothing about farming. Some of them have just taken the land but have done nothing with it. And the problem is also the British. They promised to compensate the white farmers after independence but did nothing.'

There was much more that could have been said on the subject, but we had arrived at a fork in the road. The A11 continued to the right and Philimon took a sharp left turn onto the A12. The tarred road soon gave way to gravel and wound between clusters of thatched houses on both sides. A few women could be seen tending their gardens; little children stood and stared at the car; dogs lounged in the sun and chickens focused their attention on pecking in the short grass with determination, as if this was their last meal. On our right, behind the houses, kopjes or hills of bald rock with trees and shrubs sprouting from occasional crevices rose high and dignified. Large rocks lay scattered at the feet of the kopjes, tumbled one on top of another, while colourful indigenous shrubs and wildflowers sashayed downwards like a huge rockery garden. It was warm, and the clouds had largely and surreptitiously disappeared, revealing the immense blue sky. The sun sat directly above us. We shut the windows to keep out the dust from the road. I began to feel maudlin as I stared at the beauty of the place and the women bending over their hoes, who brought back memories of my mother.

We had gone about five miles when suddenly Philimon stopped.

'I think this is where we have to turn,' he said.

I frowned.

'Here?' I remarked surprised. 'But there is no road.'

'The place is right up on top of the kopje,' Philimon said pointing to the trees, which rose higher and higher up the incline to an invisible summit. 'There is no proper road. I need to ask someone.'

A man was sitting in front of his house whittling a *tsvimbo*. He pointed the round head of the club towards a pathway, which was a series of flat rocks winding into the bushes. I wondered if Philimon would insist that we leave the car and walk the rest of the way. But he climbed in and, steering the car with the care of someone helping a toddler to walk, he negotiated the rocks and we moved slowly, bouncing in our seats until we arrived on a gravel path, which wound out of sight and upwards through the trees. The path sometimes sank into a ditch or dissolved into the bushes, but Philimon continued, guiding the car with the expertise of a tightrope walker. Finally, we arrived at the top and there, in a clearing, spread out in front of us like a vision, was a small village of about sixty little houses in neat rows nestling close to each other between musasa and other indigenous trees. A man dressed in khaki motioned Philimon to park under a tree on the edge of the village. He had heard the car straining its way up the hill and had been expecting us. He wore a leather belt, which went across his chest and over his shoulder, fastening onto another belt around his waist. On the left side of the belt hung a pouch from which was visible the handle of a large knife or dagger. I was familiar with all this and felt safe. I spoke in Shona as a mark of respect.

'Would it be possible for me to see my sister, please? She is called Filida or Amai Charles.'

Two women standing nearby had been listening and one of them immediately said, 'I'll go and fetch her.'

Philimon sat in the car, and the man in uniform disappeared among the trees and into the bushes surrounding the village. I chose a large flat rock under what looked like a young flamboyant tree without any flowers and settled myself to wait for my sister. Within a few minutes she had emerged from one of the houses at the far end of the cluster and was running laboriously towards me. She was dressed in white, as she had been since the age of twenty-three, when she had joined the cult of Mai Chaza. She was now seventy-three, but did not look a day older than fifty. I started to run towards her but she held out her hands, palms upwards and shouted, 'No, Maudie, stay there.'

Sisi Filida threw her arms around me, almost knocking me over. This was not the reserved Filida I knew. Over the years she had withdrawn further and further into herself and her religion. She stood with quiet dignity when others were dancing with joy. She always greeted me with a distant formality, even after several years of not seeing each other. She had appeared intermittently in my life when I was growing up. This time she seemed genuinely and surprisingly overjoyed to see me. She looked a little embarrassed as she took my hand and led me back to the flat rock under the tree.

Speaking in Shona, she said apologetically, 'I can't take you to my house. People who are not part of our church are not allowed past this point. But I am so glad that you have come to see where I spend most of my life.'

We chatted about family – hers, mine, and the extended family. Eventually I took out the newspaper article and without hiding the name, I showed it to her.

'Do you remember seeing this?' I asked. 'We discussed it with Sisi Margie when we came to Zimbabwe on holiday a long time ago.'

Sisi Filida took the paper and squinted at it, holding it close to her eyes.

'Mmmmm,' she said, the sound coming from her forehead. 'Ah-ah. I don't remember.'

'But do you recognise the man in the picture?'

She stared at the picture for a minute then said, 'It says Strickland, so it must be your father.'

'But does he look familiar to you?'

'No. But then he wouldn't. I never met your father.'

'What do you mean?' I almost bellowed. 'When I showed you this picture all those years ago, you told me that it was my father.'

'Aaah, did I? Are you sure it wasn't Margie who said that? She was the one who met your father, not me. I was away staying with Amaiguru Hilda and attending school at Waddilove. I met Lenning, but not Strickland. Mr Lenning was actually paying my school fees.'

'Well, it was you who didn't seem to have any doubt. Sisi Margie was the uncertain one, not you.'

'Oh, perhaps I was trying to be helpful because I knew you were desperate to find out who your father was,' she said without a trace of irony. I was not sure whether to feel relief because her words confirmed that J. C. Strickland was not my father or to weep with frustration. I stood up and said, 'I have something for you.' I walked over to the car and opened the back door, waking Philimon, who had been snoring contentedly in the front seat. I took out a box of groceries and handed it to her.

'Eeee, you've done a wonderful thing,' she said clapping her hands. 'We were running very low.'

It was time to say goodbye. I wanted to get back to Harare before dark and was not looking forward to the hazardous drive down the hill. I hugged my sister, feeling her thin back under the loose dress. I thought about the time she had come home one year when I was still at primary school and was spending time with Amai in the village. It is the one occasion in my memory in which she was dressed in something colourful. I remember feeling so proud of her. She could not have been older than eighteen or nineteen and I thought she was the prettiest young woman in the whole village. I turned away quickly and headed for the car.

Twenty-Nine

I spent many of my adult years telling myself that it did not matter if I never got to find out who my biological father was. I did not feel a sense of loss, as I had never had a father in the first place. Instead, I had had a husband and children and could give my children the kind of home I had always craved, with the lifestyle that I had only imagined when I was a child. I realise now that this dismissal of a father was out of loyalty to my mother, and that somewhere deep down I needed to know. My soul would have remained troubled unless I travelled that painful journey of discovery for myself. Inevitably this involved many hours of research; a few wrong turns; disappointment; and finally, the fear of confronting this person to whom I was linked by blood alone and yet who lived like an unfinished puzzle in the depths of my being. Without that knowledge about my father, my life would itself remain incomplete and I a fragmented being on an endless journey, forever hankering after a resolution.

My mother would have been about twenty-eight when Mrs Bhana introduced her to Mr Strickland, unaware of the life-changing course of events that such an introduction would unleash. I sometimes wondered if I had been the product of rape, given how difficult my mother found it to talk about Mr Strickland. It is of course possible that my mother was not violently forced into a sexual relationship but would have felt unable to say 'no' to the man to whom she owed her living and that of her family at a desperate time in her life. With her lack of experience of white households, it would not have been easy for her to find a job. As she barely spoke English, I surmise that he had given her the job as a favour to his friends, the Bhanas. But it probably never occurred to him to find out about her circumstances – what would provoke such a timid young African woman with very little English to leave the security of her home, her children, her mother, her friends and her village and look for a job in the daunting environment of the city, where the only people she knew were Mr and Mrs Bhana and where the bewildering culture and fast pace of life must have been terrifying to her? Did Mr Strickland know that she had children? If he had known the truth about the struggles in her life, might he have been less harsh in his treatment of her when she became pregnant?

Over the years while Sisi Margie was alive, we often talked about the trials as well as the joys that our various family members had experienced. During one of these discussions, Sisi Margie told me that my mother had been three months pregnant when Mr Strickland sent her away and warned her not to come back. This was confirmed by Sisi Tebi. I tried to understand the kind of man that would do that. Was he callous, cowardly, or both? I had struggled to understand my mother's reluctance to talk about him; to acquaint me with who he was and lift the burdensome weight of not knowing. She preferred to pretend that he had not existed. It is difficult to imagine the terror and anguish she must have felt when she found herself on the street, pregnant by a white man in an apartheid society, with no money and half a dozen other children to feed, clothe and educate. She lived in a world of white people who were hostile towards her as a black woman, and a world of black people who she feared would reject her and her mixed-heritage child. She collected her meagre belongings and walked from Borrowdale to the kopje, a distance of about fifteen kilometres, where her niece, Mrs Bhana lived with her Indian husband. Mrs Bhana had introduced her to Mr Strickland and was now the first to receive her when the arrangement failed. 'He warned her,' my sister Margie said, 'never to set foot on his property again.' My mother, a simple country woman who could neither read nor write, was hardly likely to disobey such a threat made by a white man.

When I was younger, I had felt that my mother had simply abandoned me. When I began to understand that being a Coloured was different from being an African in Rhodesia, I assumed that it was my difference that had made my mother 'cast me out'. The feeling of being unwanted stalked me for most of my life. Now, as a mother myself, I look at my children and my grandchildren and understand what it must have cost her to give me up so that I could be given an education. Only as an adult did I begin to understand the extent to which her life was circumscribed by the racial politics of Rhodesia.

The history of Rhodesia is the history of the exploitation of the indigenous black people by the white settlers. Both the amaNdebele and the Mashona rebelled against the early settlers. Both rebellions were put down by the superior firepower of the Europeans, and so began the white 'Rhodesian Way of Life', which depended on keeping Africans in a state of servitude by maintaining control over their lives. Africans were rendered poor by the dispossession of their land and powerless by the most brutal and authoritarian laws that could be devised. They were not regarded as citizens. They were disenfranchised by the high bar set to qualify for the vote, while restrictions in education and compulsory low pay meant that they could never qualify. Africans were administered separately by the Native Affairs Department, later called the Ministry of Internal Affairs, which was entirely controlled by white people.

My mother, and any African woman in her position, would have had nowhere to go for redress, even if she had had the courage to do so. Mr Strickland would surely have known this.

In 2010 Sisi Tebi, gave me four facts she said would distinguish my father from all other Stricklands, and all four, indeed five if we include his name, had to be present to ensure certainty. So the name Strickland was the first criterion. The second was that he had to have been at least sixty or older at the time of my birth. The third was that he had two sons who were already in their twenties in 1950; fourthly, he had to have been single in 1948, as there had been no evidence of a wife when Sisi Tebi went to visit my mother; finally, he had to have been living in Borrowdale, Salisbury. Sisi Tebi was unable to say whether he was English or Irish. I was forced to go back to the archives in Harare and begin the search all over again.

It was not easy to get into the archives. White people leaving the country at the time of independence had removed many documents, so that there were gaps in the information and several documents had been misfiled. Entrance was therefore restricted to academic or official research only while the stupendous task of recategorising everything electronically was carried out. It was thanks to my friend, whose father had been a respected political activist against the Rhodesian government, that I was able to get in, on the basis that I was helping her to research her father's life.

I began by searching the census and any other documents

that covered the years 1947 to 1951. There were seven Strickland families or individuals living in Salisbury at that time (including J. C. Strickland, the Irishman and Alan Strickland's brother that I had spoken with on the phone and mistakenly thought was my father). All but one young man aged twenty-three had addresses outside Borrowdale. They also lived in places that were recognisable as places in Salisbury, with the exception of one man, whom I found in the telephone directory of 1951. He was a man of indeterminate age who lived in a place – Boynton – that I had never heard of before and neither had anyone else. An inquiry at the deeds office indicated that such a place did not exist in Salisbury at the time or since. I considered the possibility that the twenty-three-year old Martin Robert Strickland might have been my brother, but I had nothing to corroborate this. The only information that linked him to the man Tebi had described as my father's son were his age and his residence in Borrowdale. After two weeks of searching, I had not found the Strickland I was after and it was time for me to go home. Back in England, I reported to my children that I had done all I could to find my father but had failed.

I had resigned myself to this when my son, who had done a search for Martin Robert Strickland on the internet, sent me a link to the Burke's Peerage website, which contained this young man's family tree. Martin Robert Strickland had a brother who was two years younger than him; his father, who was called Cecil Strickland, was born in 1889 and therefore had been sixty-one years old when I was born; he had divorced in 1942 and so did not have a wife, certainly not at the time when Sisi Tebi visited his home to see my mother. According to Burke's, he had lived in Borrowdale. Each of the five parts of the puzzle were present. There was, however, one small complication. Mr Strickland also had a daughter, born in 1951, just seven months after I was born.

In 1972, during my PGCE year, there was a white girl at the university called Jessica Strickland, who was also doing her PGCE. I was curious about her at the time because of her second name. As we were in the same year and therefore likely to be close in age, the thought came to me that she might be a cousin, but it never occurred to me that she might be my sister. My friends often teased that she was my sister and would goad me to ask her. But this was a de facto apartheid Rhodesia. Even if I had thought she was my sister, I would never have approached her for fear of an angry rejection.

The Burke's Peerage website said that C. E. Strickland had remarried in 1949. That meant Mr Strickland's relationship with my mother had happened, or had continued, six months after he married his new wife. I felt a surge of relief when I saw this. As my mother had been working for him since 1947, I felt certain that there could not have been any violence involved in my conception. She had taken the risk of leaving a violent husband and fled with five children; she was hardly going to stay four years with another violent man. There could of course have been passive force, but equally there might not have been.

A few things began to make sense to me. Despite his weakness and cowardice, I could see the difficult position in which he found himself. He stood to lose everything: possibly his new wife, his good name among his peers, the respect of his children. The boys would most likely have known what was happening. One can only wonder about the kind of conversations he might have had with them. Bringing a baby that he had with his maid into the mix might have been the death knell for his relationship with his sons. As for my mother, I began to understand her anger and her absolute refusal to talk about my birth father and her insistence on talking only about Wilfred Lenning.

Although I felt certain that this Strickland was my father,

there remained one small element of doubt. I had also been totally certain that the Irishman J. C. Strickland was my father. Could I not be making a mistake now, regardless of Tebi's five criteria? I needed to contact Mr Strickland's children, and if I was lucky, they might be willing to take part in a DNA test.

I needed courage to contact Jessica. I was afraid of a negative reaction and of the impact that would have on me. I need not have worried, because her first reaction to me, by email, was one of delight. It meant a lot to me. She was willing to have a DNA test. I also discovered that one of my potential brothers was living in America. He was less forthcoming and was both ill and elderly. Martin Robert, the young man I had found in the course of my research in Zimbabwe and the eldest of the children, had sadly died in 1983.

The DNA test was conclusive – Mr C. E. Strickland was my birth father and Jessica was indeed my sister.

There was still the mystery as to why, in the information I found about him in Zimbabwe, he lived in a place called Boynton. This, according to Jess, was the name he had given his home in Borrowdale.

Despite my understanding of his circumstances, I was angry with Mr Strickland. Neither the culture of segregation nor his marriage or children justified total abandonment. Growing up Coloured in Rhodesia, I was aware of a number of boys and girls at school who had African mothers and white fathers and, like me, did not bear their fathers' names. The difference between us was that some of them were supported by their fathers, though they were not raised by them. Some white men (albeit very few and generally a long way from the cities) lived with their African partners and were fathers to their children; some had relationships with several black women and left a trail of unsupported Coloured children in their wake, while others had several children with one black woman whom they did not live with but for whom they provided support. Such white men spanned the full gamut of livelihoods from traders to farmers, district commissioners to politicians, and many others besides.

My mother's eldest sister (Sisi Tebi's mother) was supported by her father, the notorious William Edwards, the district commissioner for Mtoko. It was said that he even wanted to take her back with him to England. The story goes that my grandmother cut large tribal scars on her face, either to make sure that she did not forget her African roots or as a deliberate ploy to make Edwards reject her. Edwards did reject her, saying that my grandmother had made his daughter look like a savage and so he would not take her to England. One girl that I went to school with was the granddaughter of a former Rhodesian prime minister. This friend's father supported her financially until well after she left school, including paying for her wedding. She did not bear his name. However cowardly and hypocritical that was, it was a form of taking responsibility.

Why then did Mr Strickland not support my mother or indeed find out about the child he had helped to bring into the world? Did he know anything about me? Did he have no curiosity? Did it never occur to him that it would be an enormous struggle for my mother, who had only gone to work for him, leaving her children with her mother, because she had no financial support for them? He had access to people who knew my mother and how to contact her. Why didn't he? My mother was a very quiet, timid person. He could hardly have felt threatened by her or any members of her family. Which African person, let alone African woman, would, at that time, have dared to threaten a white man? Rhodesia was a society ruled by white people in the interests of white people.

I could not get the answers to my questions because

Mr Strickland died in South Africa in 1981, so I sought the opinion of Sisi Tebi, whose memory and wisdom I relied on for so many things.

I telephoned Sisi Tebi on a regular basis, if only to enquire about her life. We generally ended up talking about family history. On one occasion I told her that I felt angry that Mr Strickland had left my mother to struggle and had not even bothered to find out anything about me.

'You know that your mother was not the first woman he did that to, don't you?' Sisi Tebi said.

I felt as if someone had punched me in the hollow of my chest. I was out of breath and barely able to get my words out. 'N-no, I don't know what you mean.'

'Before your mother went to work for him, he had another maid, a woman from Matabeleland. She also became pregnant. He sent her away too.'

The world around me turned into a blur; I felt numb and my head began to throb. My hand was sweating as it held the phone, and I realised that I was squeezing it hard. I could hear my heart hammering in my ears. I was silent until Sisi Tebi said, 'Are you still there?'

'Yes,' I croaked.

'Sorry about the bad news,' she said. 'But I thought you would rather know than not.'

'Yes, thank you. I would rather know. Do you know whether the child was a boy or a girl?'

'No, I don't. Mrs Bhana knew the maid, of course, but when she went back to Matabeleland, she never heard from her again.'

I had wanted so much to blame the society he lived in and to believe that he might have been weak but not callous and uncaring. The knowledge that he had put another poor black woman in such a situation made me question his character and his integrity. Given that he arrived in Africa as long ago as 1923, I began to speculate on how many others there might have been. I could have had a string of siblings for all I knew, and they would probably have been my mother's generation. No wonder my birth certificate did not state who my father was. The hypocrisy of it all was astounding. White men protecting each other. All kinds of negative epithets to describe him flooded my mind and I repeated the phrase my friend had used many years ago – 'Bladdy white men!'

I now had to go on another journey – to find my other half-sibling.

Thirty

My sister Margie and I scrutinise two old black-and-white photographs. In the first, the white man could be aged anywhere between sixty-five and seventy, tall and stringy with thinning hair and a prominent nose. His right arm is bent at the elbow and he holds what looks like a roll of tape against his midriff. Next to him is a young black boy of about fourteen. They both squint at the sun but are smiling; they have a trophy that they have suspended from a tree – an eight-foot-long python, its muscles twisted as if it were still alive. The white man is Mr Lenning.

The second photograph is of my mother and me. It appears to have been taken on the same day – the same trees in the background and the same wooden hut, probably a latrine, at some distance behind. My mother is wearing a woollen hat the shape of a bowl and sits cross-legged on the ground. I am also sitting on the ground. My mother smiles as she watches me. I must be between six and nine months old.

We talk about my childhood, Sisi Margie's memories. According to Sisi Margie, my birth led to a major rift within the family. The fact that I was the daughter of a white man caused my aunt, my mother's eldest sister, on whose farm we lived, a good deal of anxiety, even though she was herself a Coloured. She had been raised entirely in an African culture, did not go to school and spoke very little English. Furthermore, she was married to an African man and considered herself African and not Coloured. By having a child with a white man, my mother was seen to have broken the anti-miscegenation laws, and my aunt and uncle, among the few Africans who had bought a farm under the rules of the Land Apportionment Act, felt vulnerable. My aunt wanted me adopted by a Coloured family, and her daughter, Mrs Bhana, offered to take me. My aunt's mother – my grandmother – would not hear of it. This led to a bitter quarrel between my aunt and my grandmother. The relationship became untenable and my grandmother decided to move from the farm and return to her father's home in Bumburwi, near Waddilove. I was three years old.

There was possibly another explanation for the rift that wasn't to do with my birth – though my arrival may have worsened things by drawing attention to the family. When the country was divided into European land and African land, some of the good arable land was set aside for purchase by African farmers. Very few Africans had the resources for it. Their earnings were deliberately kept low so that they earned a pittance compared with white people, even for similar jobs. By 1925, Europeans had bought 31 million acres and Africans had managed to buy only 45,000 acres. My aunt, who I understand had been left some money by her white father, decided with her husband to buy one of these farms. She invited her mother, my grandmother, to live with her and gave her a portion of the farm on which she could keep her cattle. My grandmother was a successful cattle farmer and soon had a sizeable herd. In 1951 the government of Rhodesia introduced the Native Land Husbandry Act, which imposed stringent conservation measures, requiring African farmers to de-stock and modify land-tenure practices. Several African farmers lost their livelihoods as a result and had to sell their farms and seek employment in the cities. It is most likely that my grandmother, a small but feisty woman, would have refused to reduce her stock, and my aunt, fearing that she would lose her farm, would have asked her mother to conform or leave.

Sisi Margie tells me about the migration to my grandmother's paternal home – or rather, the land to which they were moved after their land, where the town of Marondera now stands, was designated for white farming and habitation. In 1953 my grandmother took her substantial head of cattle and trekked the long distance through the bush with my mother and her children – Margie, Abigail, Stan and me (Sisi Filida was in Waddilove and brother Patrick was being raised by his paternal grandmother) to Bumburwi. I remember none of this.

My mother was the youngest of six children. Her eldest sister Majeke, whose farm my grandmother vacated, was of mixed heritage. The second was a son, Dymon (I have never been able to verify whether his name was Diamond, Damian, Damon, Dynamo or, as an uncle asserted – Dynamite). He had a bad reputation for violence, lewdness – especially when drunk – and lack of respect for anyone, including the customs of the land. He is reputed to have broken some of the strictest taboos with impunity. He was feared by everybody. Agnes, quiet and reserved, was next in line, followed by Hilda, and then my mother, Serina. Agnes and Serina were very close and remained so until their deaths. Majeke, the eldest, was also very fond of Serina. Hilda was not very happy and, possibly spurred on by jealousy, bullied Serina mercilessly. Serina grew up to be timid, compliant and scared of Hilda.

When Aunt Hilda came to visit Sisi Margie and me in England in 1997, she told me that my mother had been forced to marry the younger brother of Chief Chihota, the

Paramount Chief of the area, when she became pregnant by him with Filida, my eldest sister. When Margie, their second child, was only two years old, their father left the country to find work in South Africa, where he stayed for many years and married another woman. He was reputed to have been the father of a famous African reggae musician. My mother then married a Mr Simbi and had four children – Patrick, Abigail, Stembeni and Stanley. Stembeni died of whooping cough when she was two years old. Mr Simbi was an abusive husband, which led my mother to flee to her sister's farm, where she lived for a while with her mother, my grandmother Chiraswa, before going to Salisbury to work for Mr Strickland. Aunt Hilda also told me that she had asked Mr Lenning if it was true that he was my father, as everyone believed. Mr Lenning had replied that it was not possible because he had suffered a war injury that had left him impotent. But when I was born prematurely, it was Mr Lenning who saved my life by taking me to Kutama Mission Hospital and then taking care of me and my mother until we left the area when I was about three years old. My mother never saw him again. He gave me the name Maud after his sister who lived in England, and agreed that I should also take his second name.

I had believed that Mr Lenning was my birth father because that was what my mother wanted me to believe. My mother knew very little about him. This was a time when deference to the patriarchy was such that African women in Zimbabwe did not question the power, actions or motivations of men, wherever they came from, and this was carried to its extreme when it applied to white people.

I spent many a fruitless hour searching for a Wilfred Lenning on the internet. It was while I was doing this that I remembered that conversation with my friend Jenny's mother when we concluded that we were not related because her name was spelt with an 'a', while mine was spelt with an 'e'.

She was right, not only because Mr Lenning was not my birth father, though I didn't know that then, or because of a simple misspelling. Remembering that conversation prompted me to end the search for Mr Lenning and begin a new search for Wilfred Lanning (with an 'a'!) and sure enough, he existed.

I discovered that Mr Lanning was an Englishman from Dorset and that he was born in 1884 in Kington Magna. He fought in both world wars before he went to Africa. He never married. Had my mother not told me that he was called Wilfred, I might never have found him.

In 2010, there were people in Zimbabwe who still remembered Mr Lanning. Members of my family who knew him have confirmed that he gave me the name Maud. The records I searched also confirmed that he had an older sister and that she was called Maud. So how did I come to be called Lenning instead of Lanning? This is a mistake that Zimbabweans would recognise. Black Zimbabweans then, and many still now, pronounce the open 'a' as if it were a French é. That is how Aunt Hilda would have pronounced it and the nuns in Bushtick would have written the name as they heard it.

I have often wondered what prompted an Englishman in segregated Rhodesia to claim paternity of a mixed-heritage child, thereby effectively declaring to the world that he had or was having a relationship with a black woman, despite the strength of feeling among white people about miscegenation. This is even more puzzling given that (if what Aunt Hilda told me was correct) he was impotent. In that society, most white men either denied or simply did not take responsibility for their mixed-heritage children. They certainly would not have wanted it known that they slept with black women, especially at that particular juncture in the history of Rhodesia, when a strong ideology of segregation following the South African example was imposed and practised in almost every walk of life. A few white men did take responsibility and lived with their African wives or partners, defying the social pressure they faced. My mother, speaking of Mr Lanning, once said to me, 'Your father didn't care about those rules of separation. When we travelled around the country, I sat in the front of the car and I would be holding you for everyone to see.'

In the Shona culture, biology is not the deciding factor where paternity is concerned – certainly not to the mothers. When I told my sister Margie that I had started a search for Mr Strickland, she looked at me, irritation written all over her face.

'Why?' she snapped. 'What has your father ever done for you? You should be searching for Lenning, not Strickland.'

'I just want to know who he was. There is no harm in that.'

'I think it's a waste of time and shows disrespect for Amai and for Mr Lenning. Without him you would not even have been alive today. He was your father, not Strickland.'

It was only when I explained about inheritable conditions and the implications for my children and grandchildren that Sisi Margie finally understood and relented.

This strong belief that the man who cares for you is your father probably accounts for why everyone in the family considered Mr Lanning, and not Mr Strickland, my father. It would never have occurred to any of my family who knew the truth of my paternity to talk about Mr Strickland as my father. I was fifteen years old when I was told for the first time that Mr Lanning was not my biological father. But in my head and heart, he always held that place. I have often wondered what happened to him after we left Makwiro, where he was working and where he met my mother. Some day, when the records in Zimbabwe are easier to access, I will follow the trail in the hope that he lived a happy life, surrounded by people who loved and cared for him.

Thirty-One

It has not been as good a year for mangoes in 2014 as it was the last time I visited my mother's homestead in 2012. Then, the trees seemed to sprout even more mangoes the more we picked. Today they look sparse, neglected and sad. But shade can never be rationed as long as there are trees with leaves on them. There is plenty of shade to revel in on this blistering January day.

Stan sits on a chair, his swollen gouty legs stretched out in front of him. He is sturdily built, so it comes as a shock to see him shuffle along like a man in chains, unable to lift his feet as he walks. He looks much younger than his sixty-nine years and, apart from the crease between his eyebrows – which I also have, as did our mother – there is not a line to be seen on his face. His hair has never been coloured, yet one would have to look closely to see any grey. He never did buy his bus or set up a business despite his sharp mind, burning ambition and hard work. The system finally defeated him and after a short stint in the army, where he played the trumpet in the army band, the rest of his life was one hustle after another, with nothing in the end to show for it. He and his wife now lived as subsistence farmers on the land once owned by his father, who had been the cause of my mother leaving the village.

Sisi Abigail is in her wheelchair, leaning over onto her paralysed side, as if she is about to fall over. Her face and balled-up fist bear witness to the devastation of a stroke. The paralysed right hand resembles a piece of dead wood, and her left hand grasps it as if she is afraid it might fall off her lap. This once phenomenal woman has been reduced to a vulnerable twig, dependent entirely on the goodness of her children and the generosity of others.

I saw very little of her as I was growing up but have vivid memories of a visit to her home in the township of Harare when I was about nine years old. I was very fond of her husband, a gentle hardworking man much respected by his employers at the furniture department store where he worked. I was surprised and disappointed when, some years later, I heard that they had got divorced and she had married someone else. The next time I saw her, she had settled on her own piece of land in the village, not far from our mother. There was no sign of a husband.

Sisi Filida and I sit on a reed mat on the ground. She is very thin. I cannot see her hair under her doek, but she does not look seventy-five; her dark face is smooth, devoid of blemishes or wrinkles. She is dressed, as usual, all in white from head to foot. I look at her with some envy. I find myself wondering if spending her life with the religious sect, which is like family to her, has kept her young. But I also know that her youthful looks are the limit of her good fortune. I know that the clothes she wears are the extent of her wealth. She depends for survival entirely on what she can get from her daughter and grandson and those of us able to give the occasional handout disguised as a gift. She had three children – a son and two daughters – but because of her religion and her husband's refusal to be part of it, she divorced and spent the rest of her life with her church.

'Do you realise that this is the first time that we have sat together like this, at least since I left school,' I observe.

'It's even longer than that, Maudie,' Stan says. 'Whenever you came home from school, the older ones were at work in Harare or Marondera, or they were married and living somewhere else. And then I went into the army and then went to live in other places and rarely came home. I couldn't even make it to Margie's funeral. So it might even be the first time since you were in secondary school. And now, when we have the opportunity to meet together, Margie and Patrick are no longer with us and Morsia is in England.'

'How is Morsia?' Sisi Filida asks. Stan and I had been speaking in English, which everyone understands, but Sisi Filida speaks in Shona so, like points on a railway line, we shift codes.

'She is fine,' I say. 'She had a hip operation but seems to have fully recovered.'

Sisi Abby grunts, making a sound that could be laughter or approval. She struggles to articulate, so remains silent most of the time.

'This place looks a bit sad,' I say as I observe the state of the thatch, the untidy bamboo bush and the small handful of chickens pecking nearby.

Sisi Filida looks up, defiant, as if rebuked.

'I am too old to look after it, Maudie, and I suffer from BP [blood pressure]. I am over seventy now and have no one who can help me. I need someone who can look after everything, including the cows, but it's hard to find people you can trust.'

Sisi Abigail looks up and makes another grunting noise.

On cue, Sisi Filida says, 'It's lucky that Blessing and Aubrey look after the cows.'

Sisi Abigail settles. Aubrey and Blessing are her grandsons.

They have taken responsibility not only for the care of the family cows, but also for their grandmother.

'Anyway,' says Sisi Filida. 'I have no money to pay for carers.'

A lengthy conversation ensues about the pros and cons of finding someone reliable to look after the homestead and the need to pay them. Finally, we conclude that enquiries will be made in the village for an elderly couple and I, as the only one with the means, will pay them.

I observe my siblings. Their struggle with poverty is unmistakeable; sometimes dignity has to be swallowed and they are forced to call England to ask for help so that grandchildren can be kept alive and maybe sent to school. The economy has fallen so low that the country has been turned into a hustler society. My mother's chance encounter with a white man had given me privileges that they could only dream of – our destinies determined by the measure of melanin in our skins. I steer my mind from these distressing thoughts.

'I was told that I was born under a mango tree,' I say to no one in particular. 'Is it true?'

Stan looks up, startled. 'Ah! What are you talking about, Maudie? Everybody knows that you were born at Kutama Mission.'

Sisi Abby tries to say something. She stutters and struggles, and we try to interpret.

'Well, that's what I was told,' I reply, pretending that I've understood what Sisi Abby has been trying to say.

'People like to tell lies. You shouldn't take any notice,' says Sisi Filida.

'You were the oldest,' I say. 'What do you remember?'

'I wasn't actually there at the time. I was at school in Waddilove, but everybody knows you were born in Kutama Mission.'

'But I was told that I was born prematurely and Amai

and I were rushed by Mr Lanning to Kutama after the event. Anyway, I like the idea that I was born under a mango tree and as Stan and Sisi Abby were too young to remember and you' – I say to Sisi Filida, squeezing her arm and leaning my head on her shoulder – 'you weren't there, so that's what I prefer to believe because that's what I was told.'

My siblings stare at me, unbelieving. Life in England might have many advantages, but they are not so sure about what it does for the mind! I shall probably never know the true facts about my birth, but I am sticking with the mango tree.

Sisi Filida says, 'So, Maudie. Tell us about your sister who lives in New Zealand. Did you get on with her when you went to visit?'

'Yes, we get on very well. I really like her. We are very similar in our temperaments.'

Stan's eyes skip from Sisi Filida to me.

'What sister are you talking about?'

'My father's daughter,' I say.

'But I thought that Mr Lenning had two sons. Nobody has told me about a daughter.'

'You are getting confused. Mr Strickland, my father, had two sons. Mr Lanning had no children.'

Stan is incredulous.

'But what are you telling me, Maudie? You are telling me that Mr Lenning was not your father and your father was called Strickland. Why has nobody told me this before?'

Sisi Abigail grunts and stares at me. She tries to say something. I guess correctly that she too was unaware that Mr Lanning was not my father. Stan looks unconvinced so I tell them the story of my search, with interjections from Stan like, 'But this can't be true'; 'This is unbelievable'; 'This is so strange.' He turns to Sisi Filida with an accusing look and she simply shrugs. It's clear that my news comes as a surprise to Sisi Abigail too, but I notice that her body settles from its state of tense agitation.

It is getting late. We have skipped from one subject to another, avoided any contentious topics and now we are ready to part amicably. I ask whether someone will come with me to visit our mother's grave, which is on a hillock about ten minutes' walk away, surrounded and protected by trees. Sisi Filida declines. She has to go and catch a bus to Marondera, where she lives with her grandson and his family. She has to leave right away. She hugs me gently, shakes hands with Stan and lays her hand on Sisi Abigail's withered fist, before hugging her in a rather formal and stiff way, and then goes into the kitchen to collect her bags. Stan will not be able to walk through the bushes, so he will walk to the road a few minutes away and wait for lifts to the village where he lives and from whence his father came. But he will stay with Sisi Abigail until I return.

I run most of the way to the grave. I was a sprinter once, but now even my five-year-old granddaughter can beat me in a fair race. When I arrive, I sit on the ground to steady my breath. The first time I visited my mother's grave I had felt her spirit. I had been filled with grief then. On subsequent visits, I had still felt a connection. In 2014, thirty-one years have passed since her death, and I feel empty. I try to talk to her in my mind, but it is like talking to clouds – one minute there, the next minute gone, changing shape along the way. I want to talk to her, but I am in an odd space because I have long since forgotten how to pray. For the first time ever, talking to my mother at the graveside feels silly and pointless. I stand up and touch the gravestone, then make my way back to wheel Sisi Abigail to her own home, about ten minutes' walk from my mother's homestead. I take a bus back to Harare.

Thirty-Two

The landscape has barely changed since I was a child. Groups of women are dotted along the side of the road like the mushrooms they have found in the woods. Some sell mangoes, others tomatoes, onions or sweet potatoes; the range of produce is small. Cars stop and families lean out of windows to inspect the items and to bargain, but buses rumble past like arrogant giants.

I love this land in all its familiarity, but I feel a tourist, even to my own family. I've been away too long.

I had ceased to fit comfortably into my mother's culture when I was sent away at the age of four, and incrementally lost the sense of belonging to the village community with every visit that I made. I rarely saw my mother who, when I did see her, treated me like an exotic bird that she clearly loved but over which she had been given only temporary responsibility. To the villagers I was different, 'the white man's child' with the white man's ways. At school and in the politics of the land I was given the label 'Coloured', yet even here there was something missing. The country's political and social evolution shaped the people, and there was a little corner called Coloured, and that might have been the perfect fit for me – a place of shared experiences. But my sojourns to Arcadia were few and brief, so that the distinctive culture that Coloured people forged for themselves, if only to survive, touched me like a passing breeze. One needs a connection that goes deep and dwells inside the blood. So I went to England, my father's land and that of his and therefore my ancestors, only to be redefined again and placed in a corner for 'Others'.

On the bus I look at the browns, reds and greens of the landscape and scrutinise the texture of the grass and the leaves whose smell is buried under the fumes from the bus. It is all so familiar, yet I now feel a stranger.

I recall with pain my recent visit to the social welfare department in Marondera, where I had gone to find documents relating to my registry as a 'welfare child'. A friendly receptionist had said, 'The head of the department is in his office. Just knock on the door and look inside.' I knocked a couple of times and got no reply, so I opened the door and stuck my head in. He was sitting at his desk and gave me an angry look before shooing me out with an exaggerated and hostile flick of his hand. I returned to the receptionist and she asked me to wait. I waited and waited. After about an hour, the receptionist went to the man's office. She returned and told me that he had agreed to see me.

'We don't have anything for you here,' were his first words as I entered, eyes focused on papers on his desk. I had not even shut the door behind me yet. He did not invite me to sit in one of the two guest chairs, so I remained standing.

'But I haven't even told you my name.'

'I don't need to know your name. The files are not here.'

'But I was told at the headquarters in Harare to come here.'

'We don't give them out. You have no right to them. They belong to this department.'

'I don't want to take anything away. I just want to look through them.'

'You need someone in authority to supervise and we don't have someone.'

'But I only want to look at my files, no one else's. I don't need a supervisor. I am over sixty years old.'

'I am not going to give them to you, so you can just return to America or England or wherever you have come from.'

I looked at the man, who could not have been more than forty or forty-five years old. This man who wore his official-dom like a crown was just a little boy when the country of Zimbabwe was created. Yet his hostility was as thick as a dense forest at night. I knew what he was seeing – not a Zim-babwean but a Coloured. I had experienced at least three such hostile acts in Zimbabwe since about 1990. But these were from officials. They perhaps did not want me to belong. A part of me understood the depth of hurt and anger of the African people that caused this young man, who only knew independent Zimbabwe, to dismiss me in true colonial style. Ordinary people displayed the well-known politeness, kind-ness and hospitality that Zimbabweans are so well known for. In my heart I was still a part of this country and I still had close family who loved me.

The bus rattled along on its way to Harare as I stared out at the beautiful landscape that I loved so much and that evoked so many happy memories.

I felt a sadness that I had grown up without an adult that I thought could guide me. I had been so thoroughly brainwashed into thinking that African people couldn't teach me anything that I missed out on some of the wisdom that the elders in the village, including my mother and especially Amaiguru Hilda, could have passed on to me. What I had avoided, or been deprived of by my absence, was the nurturing that came from Shona customary practices, the kind that African women in the villages were so good at. As I reflected, I realised that the separation from my mother at the age of four had left me with a deep, destructive feeling of abandonment. In primary school, I found it difficult to stay with a friend for very long. I was not bullied or unpopular, but I moved on to another friend as soon as I became close to anyone. Was this about trust? Was it a fear of abandonment? Were other mixed-race people who had had my experience affected in the same way? I will probably never know.

As we neared Harare, I decided to switch off from morbid thoughts and tried to imagine what my children were doing at that moment. I thought about my grandchildren and how avidly they listened to stories about my childhood. They were happy to hear the same stories repeatedly and never seemed to tire of them. I whispered the well-known cliché about where home is, and I was content.

I made a resolution – some day I would bring them all to visit this wonderful, confusing, frustrating, yet lovable and unique land of their ancestors.

Glossary

amai	mother
amaiguru	aunt
amaiwe	oh mother
amaNdebele	Ndebele people
ambuya	grandmother
boerewors	a type of South African sausage
chenjera imbwa	beware of the dog
chitenge	wrap-around cloth from Malawi
chongololo	millipede
dagga	marijuana
doek	headscarf
duiker	a type of antelope
the Federation	The Federation of Rhodesia and Nyasaland
hacha	monkey bread fruit (from the muhacha tree)
hondo	war

hute	fruit from the mukute tree
jana	rota of work where community members help each other e.g. tilling land, herding cattle
knobkerry	a cross between a weapon and a walking cane
kopje	small hill
kraal	enclosure
LOMA	Law and Order Maintenance Act
Machangani	Shangaan people, originally from southern Mozambique
magaka	prickly melon
maheu	fermented millet drink
matamba	monkey orange tree, also known as the Natal orange tree
mazhanje	fruit of the muzhanje tree
mealie	maize
mealie meal	ground maize
mombe	cow
mopane worm	the protein-rich caterpillar of a type of emperor moth
muhacha tree	hissing tree or mobola plum
mukoma	elder sister/brother
mukute tree	waterberry
muningina	younger sister/brother
murungu	white person
musandisiye	please don't leave me

musasa	small(ish) tree, also known as zebrawood
mutakura	bean stew
muti	informal word for medicine
mutswairo	grass broom
mwana wangu	my child
Mwari Anochema, Anotichemera isu, vana vake	God weeps, God weeps for us, his children
Ndebele	short version of either Amandebele or Sindebele
Ndinoda mombe yangu	I want my cow
n'ganga	traditional doctor
Ngozi	troubled spirits
nyimo	Bambara groundnut, a type of bean or legume
padhuze dhuze	very close by
sadza	a staple food made of ground maize
Sindebele	Ndebele language
situpa	identity card
svikiro	spirit medium
timba	African yellow warbler
tipindeiwo	literally, 'may we enter'
tsambatsi	also known as wild grape
tsenza	a root vegetable also known as the Livingstone potato
tsika	the customs and traditions of the Shona people
tsvimbo	club
varoora	outsiders who marry into a family

varungu	white people
veldt	open grassland
vetkoek	deep-fried bread bun
vlei	low lying marshland
voetsak	get lost
wona murungu dhunu	look at the albino
yowe	'oh' or 'oh my goodness'
ZANU	Zimbabwe African National Union
ZAPU	Zimbabwe African People's Union

Acknowledgements

I want to thank the following people, without whom this book might not have been written.

Julie Kavanagh and Gay Palmer, who encouraged me to write my story.

Aunt Hilda, Cousin Tabitha, sisters Margaret Crofts and Morsia Kariwo, and my brother Stanley Simbi for filling in the gaps in my memory and knowledge.

All the people who read and gave comments and encouragement. My children Michael, Mationesa, Joanna Chiraswa and WaiYin Cheung. My sister Jessica Strickland. My friends Ibbo Mandaza, Judy Monkhouse, Maggie Osborne, Helen and Roderick Snell and Ali Smith. Thank you, Ali, for directing me towards Unbound.com and thank you Elizabeth Lowe for your friendship and support throughout this journey.

Mr Alan Strickland for so graciously allowing me to use extracts from our correspondence about his family.

My editor, Vimbai Shire, whose advice, expertise and encouragement made such a big difference to the book and gave me the confidence I needed to seek publication.

My sincere thanks to all those, known and unknown,

who pledged or donated the money for publication. Special thanks to the Patrons – some of you chose not to be acknowledged, but you know who you are.

Finally, thank you to all at Unbound, but in particular, my support staff, Katy, Cassie, Aliya, Imogen, Marissa and Kate Quarry for holding my hand and taking the book on its final journey.

Unbound is the world's first crowdfunding publisher, established in 2011.

We believe that wonderful things can happen when you clear a path for people who share a passion. That's why we've built a platform that brings together readers and authors to crowdfund books they believe in – and give fresh ideas that don't fit the traditional mould the chance they deserve.

This book is in your hands because readers made it possible. Everyone who pledged their support is listed below. Join them by visiting unbound.com and supporting a book today.

Jasmin De Freitas

Sophie M Dépas

Lorena Diéguez

Adrian Dolby

Godfried Duah

Sabine Edwards

Debbie Epstein

Lynn Farley-Rose

Libby & Henry Freeland

Melanie George

David Gillborn

Catherine Grace

Heidi Green

Oli Greene

Katy Guest

Elizabeth Hakata

Michael Hakata

Rebecca Hall

Neil Harrison

Jeremy Hill

Tony Histed

Alison Hobro

Ashleigh Holmes

Gopal Hooper

Qamar Iqbal

Louise Ishani

Paul Jackson

Kasturi Jadhav

Lara Jaffey

Jacquie Jenner

Glenn Johnson

Tendai Kariwo

Julie Kavanagh

Val Kaye

John Kelt

Michael Kenworthy-Browne

Kate Khairdean

Dan Kieran

Abhilash Lal Sarhadi

W Tom Lawrie

Jessica Lissaman

Jacobus Lombard

Brian Lott

Pat Mackenzie

Kathy MacLean

Maud Masango

Barbara Mayor

Kate Mckenzie

Lois McLaren

Jennie Mead

John Meed

Carolyn Mills

Elizabeth Mitchell

John Mitchinson

Judith Monkhouse

Janet Montefiore

Cathy Moore

Fionnuala Morris

Sophie Munro

Farai Mutswunguma

Carlo Navato

Mike Neville

Sue Nieland

North Cambridge Academy

Edie O'Connor

Erin O'Connor

Juliet O'Donnell

Brian O'Neil

Eleanor O'Gorman
Laura Ormerod
M Osborn
Camilla Marie Pallesen
Steph Parker
Jane Pearce
Ann Phoenix
Justin Pollard
Hannah Postgate
Steve Reynolds
Kate Rhodes
Richard Rippin
Kate Rodwell
Sawston Village College
Lara Schneider
Vera Schuster Beesley
Hannah Settle
Sally Sines
Iram Siraj

Nigel Skellett
Toni Smerdon
Ali and Sarah Smith
    and Wood
Faye Somerville
Dylan Theodore
Thomas Thomik
Paulette Toppin
Vicky Unwin
Val Warburton
John Wates
Sophie Watson
Marianne Welle
Richard White
Rachel Williams
Tamsin Wimhurst
Joe Winter
Tom Woodcock
Rosa Wunner